EASY VEGAN BAKING

Jérôme Eckmeier
Daniela Lais

EASY VEGAN BAKING

80 easy vegan recipes

cookies, cakes, pizzas, breads, and more

CONTENTS

PREFACE

Our aim for this book was for the recipes to be quick and simple to make and, ideally, to avoid exotic ingredients. The German Vegetarian Association asked, "What vegan baking recipes would you like?" and over 600 of our Facebook friends responded. They loved wholesome foods, cookies, and muffins—and they dreamed of the perfect vegan "cheesecake."

Their careful, detailed responses show that baking is a hot topic for people who want to follow a vegan diet—whether for some or all of the time—because purely plant-based cakes, cookies, breads, and rolls are hard to find. Furthermore, information provided at bakeries isn't always reliable; for example, often you can't be sure if the margarine they use really is vegan.

So for our second book with Vegetarian Society's kitchen buddy Jérôme Eckmeier, there was never any doubt that our topic would have to be baking. Jérôme was supported on this project by our new discovery, baking expert Daniela Lais. Together, they met vegans' requests: that the recipes should be easy for anyone to follow, with clear step-by-step instructions, for example, on how to make muffins super fluffy and "cheesecake" silky smooth.

So even if you rarely venture into a kitchen, it's time to get baking! Find out how fun baking can be, how it saves money, and how it makes your home smell heavenly, too. These sweet temptations are fantastic ambassadors for veganism.

It's true that anyone who wants to bake great cakes needs a few key ingredients ... but eggs, butter, lard, and milk most definitely aren't necessary.

Yours,
Sebastian Zösch
Managing director of the German Vegetarian Association
[Vegetarierbund Deutschland e.V.]

PS
Find us at
www.vebu.de and
**facebook.com/
provegDE**

THE VEGGIE COMMUNITY TOP TEN

What is your favorite baked item—the thing you can't bear to be without, even as a vegan? A survey by the German Vegetarian Association helped identify which baking recipes the veggie community would most like while avoiding milk, eggs, and so on. The results were used as inspiration for the recipes in this book.

1. **CHEESECAKE** PP. 80–85

2. **COOKIES** PP. 38–39

3. **CUPCAKES / MUFFINS** PP. 28–33

4. **CHRISTMAS COOKIES** PP. 170–185

5. **MARBLED CHOCOLATE CHEESECAKE** PP. 54–55

6. **SPONGE CAKE** PP. 86–87; 187

7. **MARBLE CAKE (ZEBRA CAKE)** PP. 50–51

8. **BLACK FOREST GATEAU** PP. 106–107

9. **BROWNIES** PP. 34–37

10. **WAFFLES** PP. 24–25

BASIC EQUIPMENT

With tried and tested recipes; a few techniques, tricks, and skills; and the right utensils, vegan baking is just as simple as conventional baking—and sometimes even simpler.

MUST-HAVES

Liquid measuring cup, saucepans, frying pans, fine sieve/sifter, large and small spoons, paring knife or potato peeler, graters, pastry brush, cutting board, rolling pin, kitchen scales (ideally digital), toothpicks or skewer for testing. Also:

Mixing bowls

For preparing most recipes, two mixing bowls are enough. Often, dry ingredients are combined in one bowl and liquid ingredients in a second bowl. For beating cream, we also recommend a mixing bowl with a lid with an opening for the beaters.

Baking pans

High-quality baking pans made of metal or silicone are crucial for the success of many baked items. We recommend a springform pan and, where required, a pie dish, a loaf pan, a 12-hole muffin pan or silicone tray, and a rectangular ovenproof (glass) dish, for baked goods like brownies. If your baking pan isn't quite the right size, just adjust the quantities and baking times.

Parchment paper

Environmentally friendly, washable parchment paper—which can be reused again and again—or some simple coated parchment paper. Different sizes are helpful.

Electric hand whisk

For preparing cream, frostings, or toppings, at least 450-watt.

NICE TO HAVE

The decision to purchase additional kitchen gadgets is entirely up to the individual, but the items here are often highly practical, save time, and can help to make baked goods look even more attractive.

Cake ring

This holds a cake's shape during filling or stacking and helps ensure accurate alignment when there are multiple layers to a cake.

Dough scraper, spatula, and palette knife

These help smooth out the surface on creamy layers and other spreadable substances and can be used to straighten up edges.

Piping bag with nozzles

Piping bags made from reusable material are easy to use and to clean. Recommended nozzles are:
• A 14–16mm star nozzle
• A variety of 18mm nozzles for decorating cupcakes
• A flower nozzle
• A round nozzle
Adapters make it easy to change nozzles quickly by screwing and unscrewing, but you can also make a simple piping bag yourself (see p.188).

Zester or box grater

This makes it easy to remove and zest the peel on citrus fruits and shreds the zest evenly, making it ideal for decorative purposes.

Waffle iron

Use this for sweet and savory waffles—ideally, a classic heart-shaped iron. Oiling the surface makes cleaning easier.

Food processor for grinding or mixing

This is an optional luxury for preparing cakes that are made with raw ingredients or which do not involve baking. It grinds and mixes thoroughly in a single process.

PANTRY ESSENTIALS

One advantage of vegan baking is that most of the ingredients keep for longer than animal products, which can go bad very quickly. It is super easy to throw together a delicious cake with a very modest supply of high-quality, organic ingredients, which you can keep stocked in your pantry.

All-purpose flour
Shelf life: if stored in an airtight container, away from the light and in a dry location at 60.8–68°F (16–20°C), up to 1 year

Fine cane sugar
Shelf life: if stored in an airtight container, away from the light and in a dry location at 60.8–68°F (16–20°C), up to 1 year or longer

Baking powder
Shelf life: if stored in an airtight container in a dry location and unopened, 1½ years or longer

Dry yeast
Shelf life: if stored in an airtight container in a dry location and unopened, up to 2 years

Soy milk
Shelf life: kept sealed, even if not chilled, several months

Flavorless oil—for example, canola oil
Shelf life: kept sealed and airtight in a cool, dark location, at least 1 year

Vanilla extract
Shelf life: kept sealed in a cool, dark place, 6 months to 1 year. Pure vanilla extract has an indefinite shelf life

Vegan margarine
Shelf life: 6–8 weeks

"LIGHTNING" CAKES

For a 10in (25cm) long loaf pan

2½ cups	all-purpose flour, plus some extra for the pan
⅔ cup	fine cane sugar
2 tsp	baking powder
1⅛ cups	soy milk
½ cup	canola oil
1–2 tsp	vanilla extract
	margarine, for greasing the pan

Time: 5 mins prep + 1 hr baking

Preheat the oven to 350°F (180°C). Stir the dry ingredients together in a bowl. Whisk the soy milk, canola oil, and vanilla extract and add to bowl, mixing everything until smooth. Transfer the mixture to a loaf pan, greased and dusted with flour, and bake for about 1 hour, until a wooden skewer inserted into the cake comes out clean.

TIP:
Substitute ¾ cup of flour with the same quantity of ground hazelnuts, ground almonds, or coconut flakes. If desired, you can also add spices, finely chopped vegan chocolate chunks, or dried fruits from your pantry supplies.

9

KNOW-HOW—TECHNIQUES, TIPS, AND TRICKS

In order to avoid eggs, milk, and cream, vegan baking has to use other ingredients to strengthen and stabilize baked goods and to create light, moist, and tasty dishes. With the right ingredients and techniques, this is not a problem.

Vinegar as a catalyst

Cider vinegar is best for vegan baking. You won't be able to taste the vinegar at all in the finished cake, but it helps the baking soda unleash its power and, when combined with soy milk, it improves the quality of the baked product. Whisk soy milk and vinegar together in a bowl; the acetic acid thickens the soy milk after about 5 minutes. Stir the mixture into your other ingredients to make light cakes and pastries with a fine texture.

Mixing with a spoon

With many vegan recipes, it is important not to "overstir" the mixture, so ingredients should be mixed gently with a spoon. The carbon dioxide in mineral water can potentially make the mixture lighter and fluffier, and the addition of leavening agents, such as yeast and baking soda, also help the dough rise and lighten beautifully. Mixing with an electric mixer or stirring for too long or too vigorously would destroy the resulting air bubbles, making the dough too heavy and stopping it from rising properly. Mixtures should not be left to stand for too long after stirring; instead, they should be baked promptly, as soon as the leavening agents have been allowed to work fully, so that the mixture rises well. Any fillings, such as fruit, should be washed and chopped before preparing the mixture so they can be added quickly.

Sweeten properly

Always use fine cane sugar. Coarse cane sugar is best avoided, as it doesn't dissolve easily, particularly in pie dough. Coarse sugar can impede or even completely prevent the mix from rising. In dark mixtures prepared with lots of cocoa powder, coarse cane sugar crystals can remain visible—indicating that the sugar has failed to dissolve. This means the sugar won't evenly sweeten the baked item.

Gelling and setting

Agar-agar is a good plant-based gelling agent, most commonly available in powdered form. Since it has powerful bonding capabilities, it is used very sparingly: ½ tsp agar-agar is enough for about 1⅛ cups liquid. The fine powder is stirred into cold liquid, which is briefly brought to a boil, simmered for a few minutes, then quickly stirred into the mixture that needs to set. The liquid will only set once it has cooled down completely. Alcohol reduces the setting properties, as do citrus fruits and their juices, due to their acidity.

Whipping cream

Always make sure your soy, rice, or coconut whipping cream is well chilled, and beat it at high speed using an electric hand mixer for at least 3 minutes, until the cream is nice and stiff. Rice cream is less firm in consistency after whisking than soy or coconut cream, so, if using this, we recommend you sprinkle in some cream stiffener about halfway through whisking before continuing to beat. If the cream is chilled again after beating, it will set even more firmly and is particularly good for piped decorations.

Oven temperatures

Unless otherwise specified, the temperatures in this book refer to nonconvection settings. For convection ovens, the temperature should be lowered by about 68°F (20°C).

SIMPLY VEGANIZED

Nowadays, most animal products can easily be replaced with plant-based equivalents, sometimes by simply combining two or three ingredients with each other.

Butter	Vegan margarine
Buttermilk	1 part soy milk + 1 part soy yogurt + 1 splash lemon juice
Cream	Soy cream, rice cream, coconut cream, or oat cream
Cream cheese	Mix 1lb 2oz (500g) soy yogurt with 14oz (400g) cashews in a high-powered blender or food processor until you have a fine, creamy purée. Transfer to a bowl, cover securely with plastic wrap, and leave to ferment at room temperature for 24 hours.
Gelatin	Agar-agar
Honey	Agave syrup or maple syrup
Milk	Soy milk, oat milk, almond milk, spelt milk, rice milk, hemp milk, or other nut milks
Quark	Soy quark or silken tofu. Alternatively, line a sifter with a clean linen cloth and place it over a bowl. Add unsweetened soy yogurt, then twist the ends of the cloth together firmly at the top, holding them in place with a rubber band. Place in the refrigerator overnight and squeeze out any excess liquid.
Sour cream	1 part soy yogurt + 1 part soy cream + 1 splash lemon juice, or alternatively, finely puréed silken tofu
Whipped egg whites	Ener-g Egg Replacer
Yogurt	Soy yogurt

INSTEAD OF 1 EGG

There are various options for replacing eggs, but the ingredients should always be chosen to suit the flavor of the relevant recipe.

1 tsp egg substitute powder + 3½ tbsp water (follow instructions on pack)

¼ cup unsweetened applesauce

1 tbsp chickpea flour mixed with 2 tbsp water

½ a large, very ripe banana, finely mashed

1 tbsp ground flax seed mixed with 3 tbsp water; leave to stand for 10 minutes—only use for dark mixtures because the brown dots will be visible in pale mixtures

1 tbsp soy flour mixed with 2 tbsp water—rule of thumb: replaces up to 3 eggs

BRIEF PRODUCT INFORMATION

Agar-agar is a plant-based alternative to gelatin made from algae and mainly available in powder form. Agar-agar is completely tasteless.

Agave syrup is a sweetener that is free from commercial industrial sugar and can be used as a 1:1 substitute for honey. Agave syrup has a slightly less intense flavor than maple syrup.

Baking soda (sodium hydrogen carbonate) is a leavening agent that is an ingredient in baking powder (which also contains an additional acidifier). Baking soda only takes effect when it is combined with acidic ingredients, such as vinegar or lemon, and it helps to make cakes light and fluffy.

Cheese is often used in savory baking recipes. Vegan brands of cheese available in the US with good melting properties include Tofutti, Daiya, Miyoko's Kitchen, and Kite Hill.

Egg substitute products are powders you can buy that are made from starch and thickening agents.

Fine cane sugar has the best baking properties; it has a subtle caramel flavor and is pleasantly sweet. It is produced by squeezing out the sugar cane and boiling the juice to make a syrup to which tiny sugar crystals are added. These are then cleaned and dried. Alternatively, coconut sugar, xylitol, or stevia can be used. The important thing to remember is: don't just substitute sugar 1:1 with agave syrup or maple syrup. The mixture would end up having very different properties if you did this.

Flax seeds are the mature seeds from the flax plant (also known as flaxseed) and should always be freshly ground, as they easily go rancid if stored for long periods. Flax seed is very high in fat, so it shouldn't be ground in a flour mill. It is also available for sale already ground.

Flour is all-purpose in most recipes. Whole-wheat flours have more vitamins, fiber, and minerals than more refined white flours. However, you shouldn't simply use whole-wheat flour as a substitute for white flour, because whole-wheat flour generally requires about 10 percent more liquid. Some people cannot tolerate the gluten that is present in spelt, einkorn, emmer, green spelt, barley, oats, kamut, rye, triticale, or wheat. Gluten-free flour mixtures are available in well-stocked supermarkets and stores.

Guar gum is used in vegan baking and cooking as an egg substitute, a gelling agent, and a plant-based thickening agent. It is obtained from the seeds of the guar bean.

Maple syrup is another sweetener that is a good substitute for honey. Maple syrup is primarily used in recipes for sweets or breakfast foods, such as brownies or pancakes.

Margarine that is suitable for vegans is produced using palm oil, coconut oil, sunflower oil, or soy. Most vegan varieties of margarine have excellent baking properties, but some have a very high water content and should not be used for baking. A good margarine should have an original buttery taste and a nice consistency. Here, again, it's important to pay attention to the information on the package.

Oils, particularly organic oils, often have a very intense flavor. For baking, you should use high-quality, flavorless baking oils so that the taste of the oil doesn't overpower the other flavors in the cake. Ideal choices for baking include canola oil, sunflower oil, and corn oil.

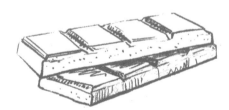

Psyllium husks are the husks of the small, dark, shiny seeds of the Indian psyllium plantain. The husks contain high levels of swelling agents and mucilage, so they are used as a plant-based swelling agent.

Silken tofu has a soft, gel-like consistency and is ideal for combining with other ingredients for baking.

Soy and soy products should be purchased carefully. Select organic soy products made from non-GMO soy beans. If it's possible to find the information, look for ones that haven't been transported over huge distances.

Soy cream/soy cream substitutes, like rice or oat creams, are not generally suitable for whipping, but are used for spreading or making a ganache. Cream substitutes specifically for whipping—made from soy, rice, or coconut—are also available. After whipping, rice cream has a slightly less firm consistency than soy or coconut cream, so we recommend the addition of some cream stiffener here. In contrast to the animal products, plant-based creams cannot be "overbeaten."

Soy flour is a dried product obtained from the soy bean and cannot simply be replaced by other flours, as none have the binding capacity of soy flour. Choose soy flour that is labeled "full fat," and never store it beyond the specified use-by date because it can easily go rancid.

Soy milk, nowadays, comes in numerous varieties. Some are unsweetened, others are sweetened or include vanilla or chocolate flavoring, and many more besides. You can use any of these, but it is important to avoid ending up with a baked product that is too sweet or has overly dominant flavors. Savory baked items are always prepared with unsweetened soy milk. Often, for successful vegan baking, it is essential to thicken the soy milk using vinegar; on no account should you substitute other milks for the soy milk in this case. If you are just starting out on a vegan diet, it is best to chill soy milk well before drinking and select a slightly sweetened version to get used to the rather different milk flavor.

Soy yogurt is best unsweetened for baking. If you are using already-sweetened soy yogurt or a variety with added vanilla flavoring, you will need to be careful that your mix doesn't end up too sweet and that the vanilla flavor is not too dominant.

Starch is used in some recipes for binding. Unless specified otherwise, cornstarch is intended.

Vanilla can be bought in different forms. You can buy vanilla beans, which are split open lengthwise and the seeds scraped out using a knife. Vanilla beans are very expensive, so the seeds should be used sparingly. The pods can also be ground and finely pulverized, then added to your baking ingredients. Ground vanilla can be obtained as a store-bought product, and vanilla beans can be stored in a jar of sugar to create "vanilla" sugar. You can also buy vanilla extract—vanilla flavoring—in liquid form.

WHAT'S WHAT—PASTRY, DOUGH, ICING, AND TOPPINGS QUICKLY EXPLAINED

Batter: The ingredients in these mixtures are simply stirred together. If desired, you can then fold in fruit or berries, or some vegetables for savory cakes.

Chocolate ganache: A chocolate ganache is made from a combination of chocolate and cream. Dark chocolate is finely chopped, melted, and stirred into a plant-based cream until smooth. The ganache is then spread over the cake or tart. A tip here: tilt the tray or baking pan so that the ganache can run evenly over the surface; this avoids leaving visible spoon marks when you are finished. Moist substances, such as a cream layer, should be thoroughly chilled before spreading the ganache, and the chocolate ganache itself should not be too hot when it is applied.

Cookie dough: Cookie dough is usually made with lots of eggs. In vegan baking, it is made without eggs but still manages to be fluffy and moist. Pale cookies usually contain mineral water plus vanilla as a flavoring; darker cookies contain soy milk and cocoa powder for coloring. Baking powder and baking soda work in conjunction with acids (for example, from a lemon) to act as leavening, or raising, agents.

Cupcakes: In contrast to muffins, these usually have a sugary-sweet, creamy frosting. They can be decorated creatively and are a great dessert to bring with you to an event.

Frosting: Margarine, powdered sugar, and a liquid are the main components in the frosting found on cupcakes or larger cakes. It is crucial that the individual ingredients are all the same temperature when being prepared. The margarine is beaten until fluffy, then powdered sugar is sifted and beaten into the mix, and finally a liquid (such as syrup, or even a jam or fruit purée) is gradually added and carefully folded in.

Icing: For icing or a glaze, sifted powdered sugar is stirred into a liquid. This works best with lemon juice. In order to produce a viscous, opaque, beautifully white icing, the lemon juice should only be added to the powdered sugar one spoon or drop at a time and stirred until smooth. If the icing is going to be scattered with nuts or other decorations, this needs to be done relatively soon after the icing has been spread because it dries quickly.

Phyllo pastry: Phyllo pastry consists mainly of finely sifted flour, water, and fat. Ideally, the phyllo pastry should be so thin, you can almost see through it. The art is in working with the pastry without ripping it. You can also buy store-bought phyllo pastry, which is often vegan.

Pie dough: Pie dough is often used when making cookies, cheesecakes, or pies that have a filling. It can be pale or dark and is usually made from flour, sugar, baking powder, margarine, and possibly some water.

Puff pastry: Puff pastry is a laminated dough consisting of multiple layers which puff up on baking (hence the name). The main ingredients are flour, salt, and water, with butter (or margarine for vegan baking) incorporated in several stages. Store-bought puff pastry from the supermarket is usually vegan and is excellent for baking strudel dishes.

Yeast doughs: Consists of flour, some salt and sugar, water or soy milk, yeast, and sometimes some oil or margarine. Temperature plays an important role when preparing yeast doughs: the temperature of the liquid that the yeast is dissolved in should be around 90°F (32°C) to enable the yeast to dissolve and let the dough rise properly. Working with dried yeast is slightly easier, as this can be stirred straight into the flour mixture.

WHERE TO FIND IT

Nowadays, you can find vegan products in every well-stocked supermarket, not to mention your local organic store or health food store. Other options include vegan (mail-order) retailers, and often Asian and Turkish food stores as well. Occasionally, products that are labeled as "vegan" do in fact contain nonvegan ingredients, but this can generally be discovered from the packaging details. Read carefully and, if in doubt, ask the manufacturer!

EASY SHOPPING—VEGAN STYLE

	Supermarket	Organic store	Health food store	Vegan (mail-order) retailers
Agar-agar		×	×	×
Agar nectar	×	×	×	
Maple syrup	×	×	×	×
Cider vinegar	×	×	×	
Puff pastry/phyllo pastry	×	×		×
Egg substitute powder		×	×	×
Vegetarian cream cheese		×	×	×
Vegetarian cocoa powder	×	×	×	×
Vegetarian cheese		×	×	×
Vegetarian margarine	×	×	×	×
Vegetarian milk (soy, oat, almond, rice)	×	×	×	×
Vegetarian quark				×
Vegetarian cream (soy, rice, oat)	×	×	×	×
Vegetarian cream, for whipping		×	×	×
Vegetarian sour cream		×		×
Vegetarian chocolate	×	×	×	×
Silken tofu		×	×	×
Soy yogurt	× (refrigerated section)			× (and other plant-based yogurts)
Soy/chickpea flour	× (chickpea flour)	×	×	×
Vanilla, powder	×	×	×	

SWEET BITES

For breakfast, dessert, or a snack: a delicious start to the day, ideal for cookie monsters or those with a sweet tooth, and great to take along to a party.

POWER BAR
WITH MORINGA

This healthy bar gives you an instant energy boost thanks to the nutritious goji berries, high-protein moringa powder, and sweet dried fruit.

For a 8 × 8in (20 × 20cm) pan (12–16 bars)

6oz (175g)	whole almonds
3¼oz (90g)	dried apricots
3½oz (100g)	dates (ideally Medjool)
2 tbsp	agave syrup
½	seeds scraped from vanilla bean
1¾oz (50g)	goji berries
1 tbsp	moringa powder (from a health food or vegan store)
¼ tsp	sea salt

Time: 15 mins prep + 1 day soaking

1 A day in advance, soak the almonds in cold water. Soak the apricots about 30 minutes before starting preparation, then drain. Purée the almonds, apricots, dates, agave syrup, and vanilla seeds in a food processor to create a paste. Scrape the paste from the sides of the container between pulses with a spatula.

2 Transfer the paste to a bowl; stir in the goji berries, moringa powder, and sea salt; and combine everything to make a cohesive mixture. Transfer the mixture to a pan lined with parchment paper and press the mixture flat. Leave to chill thoroughly, then cut into bars.

TIP:

The power bars will keep for about 2 weeks if stored in an airtight container in the refrigerator, so they are ideal for preparing in larger quantities so that you can stock up on your supply of them.

These soft, round rolls are a delicacy that taste best if eaten fresh from the oven, either plain or with some vegan margarine and jam.

BRIOCHE ROLLS

Makes 10 rolls (or 10in/1 × 25cm loaf pan)

Time: 10 mins prep + approx. 5 hrs proofing + 30 mins baking

1¾ cups	all-purpose flour, plus some more for dusting
1 tsp	dried yeast
¼ cup	fine cane sugar
1	pinch of salt
½	seeds scraped from vanilla bean
2 tbsp	vegan margarine, plus some more for greasing
3½ tbsp	soy milk, for brushing
¼ cup	powdered sugar, for dusting

1 In a large bowl, mix together the flour, dried yeast, cane sugar, and salt. Fold in the vanilla seeds. Add ½ cup water and knead for about 5 minutes. Then add the margarine and knead again—it will take a while for the dough to absorb the fat. Cover and leave the dough to proof in a warm place for 45 minutes, until it has doubled in size.

2 To knock out the air from the dough, use your hands to gently work the dough into a ball. Leave it covered in the refrigerator for at least 3 hours, or ideally overnight. Then create 10 equal-sized rolls from the dough and place them on a baking sheet lined with parchment paper. Alternatively, grease a loaf pan and dust it with flour. Place the dough in the pan and smooth it out. Cover the rolls or the bread with a clean, damp kitchen towel and leave to rise for 1 hour, until the dough has doubled in volume.

3 Preheat the oven to 350°F (180°C). Brush the rolls or bread with soy milk. Bake the rolls for 15–20 minutes, or the bread for 25–30 minutes, in the center of the oven until golden. Leave to cool slightly and dust with powdered sugar.

Delicious and fluffy, these pancakes are a guaranteed breakfast highlight. They are traditionally eaten with maple syrup or fresh fruit.

ALL-AMERICAN PANCAKES

Makes 4 pancakes

Time: 15 mins prep + cooking

For the batter:

1 cup	all-purpose flour
1 tsp	baking soda
1	pinch of salt
½ cup	soy milk or almond milk
4oz (115g)	soy yogurt
1 tbsp	canola oil

Also:

flavorless oil, for cooking

maple syrup, fresh fruit, vegan chocolate chips, or jam, to serve

1 In a bowl, combine the flour with the baking soda and salt. In a separate bowl, mix together the soy or almond milk, soy yogurt, 2 tablespoons of water, and the canola oil.

2 Use a spoon to quickly fold the liquid ingredients into the dry mixture until you have a smooth, stiff batter. Heat some oil in a pan. Put dollops of about 3 tablespoons of the batter into the oil and gently smooth them down into pancakes. (Don't press them completely flat; they are supposed to be slightly thick.) Cook the pancakes over medium heat, adding some more oil if necessary. Once the pancakes are pale brown on one side, flip them over and cook on the other side.

3 Serve the pancakes immediately, with plenty of maple syrup and fresh fruit, chocolate chips, jam, or whatever you like.

TIP:

The pancakes can be served as a perfect hearty weekend breakfast, layered up with baked beans and some tofu sausages on the side. For a sweet morning treat, drench the pancakes in maple syrup and garnish with slices of banana.

These vegan, soy-free waffles can be served with a fruit purée, jam, or simply powdered sugar for a breakfast treat or for afternoon coffee with friends.

FLUFFY WAFFLES

Makes 6–8 waffles

Time: 15 mins prep + cooking

For the batter:

2¾ cups	all-purpose flour
¼ cup	fine cane sugar
2 tbsp	baking powder
½ tsp	salt
3 cups	rice milk
⅓ cup	orange juice, freshly squeezed
1–2 tsp	vanilla extract
⅓ cup	canola oil
1	generous splash of rum

Also:

vegan oil spray (or vegan margarine), for greasing the iron
jam, fresh fruit, powdered sugar, or whipped soy cream (as desired), to serve

1 To make the batter, combine the flour, cane sugar, baking powder, and salt in a bowl. In a separate bowl, whisk the rice milk with the orange juice and vanilla extract and leave to thicken for 5 minutes, then add the canola oil and rum and stir all of the liquid ingredients together until smooth.

2 Combine the liquid and dry ingredients to create a smooth batter. The batter shouldn't be left to stand for too long, so use it quickly.

3 Preheat the waffle iron and spray it generously with an oil spray. Add a ladle of batter to the iron and cook. Repeat to make one waffle after another. Carefully remove the waffles from the iron and serve immediately with jam, fresh fruit, powdered sugar, and/or soy cream.

TIP:
These fabulously fluffy waffles, made without any soy flour or egg substitute, are even more flavorful with the addition of vanilla powder to the batter. If serving to children, leave out the rum.

PUDDING PRETZELS

Makes 8–10 pretzels

Time: 40 mins prep + 65 mins proofing + 20 mins baking

For the dough:

2½ cups	all-purpose flour
2 tbsp	fine cane sugar
	pinch of salt
2 tsp	dried yeast
2 tbsp	vegan margarine
¾ cup	soy milk
9½oz (270g)	puff pastry (store-bought; see pp.14–15)

For the filling:

2 cups	vanilla soy milk
2oz (60g)	instant custard powder
½	seeds scraped from vanilla bean
⅓ cup	fine cane sugar
	pinch of salt
2 tbsp	vegan margarine

For the icing:

1 cup	powdered sugar
	squeeze of lemon juice

1 To make the dough, mix the flour, cane sugar, salt, and yeast in a bowl. Melt the margarine and add to the dry ingredients along with the soy milk. Knead everything to form a smooth dough, cover, and leave to proof in a warm place for about 45 minutes, until it has doubled in size.

2 Roll out the yeast dough to the same size as the puff pastry sheet (approx. 16 × 9½in/42 × 24cm). Place the dough sheet on top of the puff pastry sheet and prick all over with a fork. Fold the sheet over once and roll it out again, then cut into ¾in (2cm) wide strips. Twist each strip as tightly as possible and form a pretzel shape with it. Place the pretzels on a baking sheet lined with parchment paper, cover, and leave to proof in a warm place for 20 minutes. Preheat the oven to 350°F (180°C) and bake the pretzels on the middle shelf for 20 minutes. Remove from the oven and leave to cool completely.

3 For the filling, mix ¾ cup of the soy milk with the custard powder until smooth. Place the remaining soy milk in a pan and bring to a boil over medium heat, adding the vanilla seeds, cane sugar, and salt. Remove the pan from the heat and add the custard powder mix, then bring to a boil again, stirring constantly. Take the pan off the heat once more, add the margarine, and stir until smooth. Leave it to cool.

4 To make the icing, sift the powdered sugar into a bowl, then stir in a bit of water and lemon juice until you have a smooth, thick mixture. Coat the pretzels with the icing. Put the custard filling into a piping bag with a large star nozzle attached and pipe it into all the hollow spaces of the pretzels.

These cupcakes are great to take to a party or just enjoy as a stunning and delicious treat.

BLUEBERRY CUPCAKES
WITH FRUITY FROSTING

Makes 12 cupcakes

Time: 35 mins prep + 25 mins baking

For the cupcakes:

1¾ cups	spelt flour
¾ tsp	baking powder
¾ tsp	baking soda
½ tsp	salt
½ cup	soy milk
	juice and zest of
1	small organic lemon
½ cup	agave syrup
2	large, very ripe bananas
9oz (250g)	blueberries (frozen or fresh), plus
3½oz (100g)	blueberries, for decoration

For the frosting:

11 tbsp	soft vegan margarine
4 cups	powdered sugar
3–4 tbsp	blueberry syrup

1 To make the cupcakes, mix the flour with the baking powder, baking soda, and salt in a bowl. In a separate bowl, stir together the soy milk and the lemon juice and zest and leave to thicken for about 5 minutes. Stir in the agave syrup. Peel the bananas and mash well using a fork. Add the bananas to the soy milk and agave syrup mixture and stir everything well. Stir the liquid ingredients into the dry ingredients. Finally, carefully fold in the blueberries.

2 Preheat the oven to 350°F (180°C). Put paper liners into the wells in a muffin tray and divide the mixture between the liners. Bake the cupcakes in the center of the oven for 20–25 minutes, until a skewer inserted into a cupcake comes out clean. Remove from the oven and leave to cool completely.

3 To make the frosting, use an electric mixer on its highest setting to beat the margarine until it is creamy. Sift the powdered sugar into the margarine and continue to beat until well combined, then carefully stir in the blueberry syrup to create a smooth cream. Transfer into a piping bag with a star nozzle attached. To do this, fold over the end of the piping bag and hold the bag low, then fill with the icing. Scrape down the contents, making sure there is no air in the bag. Pipe swirls of frosting onto the cupcakes. Decorate the swirls with blueberries. If you prefer a little less sweetness, reduce the frosting ingredients by half.

TIP:

You can also make these cupcakes with other fruits, such as raspberries. Replace the blueberry syrup with raspberry syrup, too.

HAZELNUT CUPCAKES
WITH CHESTNUT AND VANILLA FROSTING

Makes 12 cupcakes

Time: 40 mins prep + 25 mins baking

For the cupcakes:

1¾ cups	all-purpose flour
1⅓ cups	ground hazelnuts
¾ cup	fine cane sugar
1½ tsp	baking powder
1⅛ cups	vanilla soy milk
½ cup	canola oil

For the frosting:

1⅛ cups	soy milk
3 tbsp	cornstarch
2–3 tsp	vanilla extract
¼ cup	fine cane sugar
7 tbsp	soft vegan margarine, beaten until creamy
1½lb (675g)	chestnut purée
3 tbsp	rum
3–4 tbsp	powdered sugar

For the filling:

1 cup	soy cream, suitable for whipping, well chilled
1 tsp	cream stiffener
½ cup	cranberry jam or hazelnut praline, plus extra for decorating
	some vanilla powder, for the nutty filling

1 Preheat the oven to 350°F (180°C). To make the cupcakes, combine the flour, ground hazelnuts, cane sugar, and baking powder in a bowl. In a separate bowl, whisk together the soy milk and canola oil. Add the liquid ingredients to the dry ingredients and combine.

2 Put paper liners into the wells of a muffin tray and fill evenly with the mixture. Bake the cupcakes in the center of the oven for about 25 minutes.

3 Meanwhile, make the frosting by cooking the soy milk, cornstarch, vanilla extract, and cane sugar in a pan over medium heat, stirring constantly, until you have a custard, then leave to cool. Beat vigorously with an electric mixer, then stir in the margarine. Add the chestnut purée and rum, sift over the powdered sugar, and stir everything together until you have a smooth frosting.

4 For the filling—both the fruity and the nutty version—whip the cream with some cream stiffener. For the fruity version, sir in the jam; for the nutty version, stir in the hazelnut praline and vanilla powder.

5 Use a tablespoon to scoop out a slight hole in each cupcake (ideally in a single piece), put in some of the filling, then pop the piece of cupcake you hollowed out back on top. Transfer the frosting into a piping bag with a round nozzle attached and pipe swirls on top of the cupcakes. Decorate each one with some jam or finely chopped hazelnut praline.

If you like cupcakes and strudel, you will fall in love with this exquisite creation, which combines juicy fruits, delicate spices, and soft vanilla cream.

STRUDEL CUPCAKES

Makes 12 cupcakes

Time: 35 mins prep + 30 mins baking

For the cupcakes:

9oz (250g)	phyllo pastry (store-bought; see pp.14–15)
6 tbsp	vegan margarine
¾ cup	whole-wheat breadcrumbs
¼ cup	fine cane sugar
1lb 2oz (500g)	apples or pears, plus extra for decorating rum (optional)

For the topping:

1 cup	soy cream, suitable for whipping, well chilled
2 tsp	cream stiffener
1	seeds scraped from vanilla bean
1 tsp	vanilla extract (optional)

1 For the cupcakes, first put paper liners into the wells of a muffin tray. Cut a total of 24 squares from the phyllo pastry. Melt the margarine in a small pan over medium heat and use this to brush the pastry pieces on all sides, leaving some margarine remaining. In each muffin pan well, lay 2 squares on top of one another with the points angled so that it looks a bit like a star. Carefully press the pastry right down into the base and sides of each well.

2 Preheat the oven to 350°F (180°C). Add half of the remaining margarine to a pan, heat it once again, and sauté the breadcrumbs in it. Transfer to a bowl and mix with the sugar, then set aside. Peel and core the apples or pears and chop into little cubes. Fold the diced fruit into the breadcrumb and sugar mixture and drizzle with rum, if using.

3 Divide the fruit evenly between the muffin wells; it is fine to pile it up a bit. Fold the corners of the pastry over the top, press down, and brush with some margarine. Bake the cupcakes in the center of the oven for about 30 minutes, until golden brown. Remove from the oven and leave to cool completely.

4 For the topping, beat the cream with the cream stiffener, vanilla seeds, and vanilla extract, if using. Top the cupcakes with the cream and decorate with a piece of apple or pear before serving.

TIP:

To prevent the decorative fruit pieces from going brown, drizzle them with some lemon juice or brush with clear vegan jelly.

Really sinful—that's how brownies should be! Savor the intense chocolate flavor and creamy consistency. When combined with peanuts, the result is an unrivaled little chocolate indulgence.

BROWNIES WITH A PEANUT KICK

For a 8 × 8in (20 × 20cm) baking pan

Time: 30 mins prep + 45 mins baking

For the brownie mix:

7 tbsp	soft vegan margarine
1 cup	fine cane sugar
6oz (175g)	silken tofu
1 cup	all-purpose flour
1	seeds scraped from vanilla bean
½ cup	vegan cocoa powder
1 tsp	baking powder
1	pinch of salt
¼ cup	soy milk
½ cup	crunchy peanut butter
¼ cup	maple syrup
5 tbsp	roasted peanuts
2oz (60g)	vegan dark chocolate

For the topping:

5½oz (150g)	vegan dark chocolate
1 tsp	coconut oil
3 tbsp	smooth peanut butter

1 Preheat the oven to 350°F (180°C). Line the baking pan with parchment paper. To make the brownie mixture, beat the margarine until creamy using an electric mixer on its highest setting, gradually adding the sugar while beating. Squeeze out the silken tofu slightly and dab dry with some paper towel, then stir into the margarine and beat everything until you have a cohesive mixture.

2 In a separate bowl, combine the flour, vanilla seeds, cocoa powder, baking powder, and salt, then fold this into the margarine and tofu mixture. Mix the soy milk with 3 tablespoons of the crunchy peanut butter and the maple syrup, then gradually stir this into the brownie mixture. Finally, chop the peanuts and dark chocolate and fold these in, too.

3 Put half the mixture into the pan and smooth it out, then put little blobs of the remaining crunchy peanut butter over the mixture before covering with the rest of the brownie mix. Smooth the surface and bake in the center of the oven for about 45 minutes. Remove from the oven, leave to cool completely, and cut into 6–9 brownies.

4 Transfer the brownies to a wire rack with greaseproof paper under it. To make the topping, melt the chocolate and coconut oil over a double boiler, stirring carefully, then spread this over the brownies. Don't worry if the chocolate runs down the sides a bit. Gently heat the smooth peanut butter and use a teaspoon to carefully make 3 little blobs, spaced slightly apart, on the still-warm chocolate. Finally, take a fairly thick wooden skewer and pull it through each blob to create a heart shape.

Brownies taste great when prepared with lots of cocoa powder, sugar, and fat, but this quickly prepared chilled version is also fantastic. Try it out sometime!

RAW ALMOND BROWNIES

For a 10 × 10in (25 × 25cm) baking pan

Time: 25 mins prep + 1 day soaking + 3 hrs chilling

For the brownies:

14oz (400g)	whole almonds
3½oz (100g)	raisins
7oz (200g)	cocoa nibs (roasted pieces of cocoa bean; from a health food store or organic supermarket)
1 cup	cocoa powder
¼ cup	maple syrup
2 tbsp	baobab powder (from a health food store, vegan supermarket, or online retailer)
6 tbsp	coconut oil

Also:

unsweetened coconut flakes, for sprinkling

1 A day in advance, soak the almonds in plenty of water. Drain the almonds thoroughly, then grind them coarsely in a food processor. Add the remaining ingredients and process everything until you have a uniform mixture.

2 Sprinkle the base of the cake pan with coconut flakes. Transfer the mixture to the pan and smooth it out. Leave to stand for about 2–3 hours in the refrigerator, then turn it out onto a cutting board and cut into 9–12 pieces.

TIP:
If the mixture is too dry and heavy, add some more water.

CHOCOLATE CHIP COOKIES
THE SALTY WAY

Makes 10–12 cookies

5 tbsp	vegan margarine
⅓ cup	fine white cane sugar
⅓ cup	fine brown cane sugar
	seeds scraped from
1	vanilla bean
½ cup + 2 tbsp	all-purpose flour
½ tsp	salt
½ tsp	baking soda
1¼oz (40g)	ground almonds
2¾oz (80g)	vegan dark chocolate, finely chopped

Time: 20 mins prep + 10 mins baking

1 In a large bowl, beat the margarine with an electric mixer until creamy. Add the white and brown cane sugar and beat everything on the highest setting for several minutes, then stir in the vanilla seeds.

2 In a separate bowl, combine the flour, salt, baking soda, and almonds. Gradually stir this into the fat and sugar mixture until you have a consistent dough. Finally, fold in the chocolate with a spoon so that it is evenly distributed.

3 Preheat the oven to 350°F (180°C). Using 2 teaspoons, cut off little portions of the dough and put them on a baking sheet lined with parchment paper. Take care to leave a gap between them, as the dough will spread out slightly as it bakes.

4 Bake the cookies in the center of the oven for about 10 minutes. When the edges are golden brown, remove the cookies from the oven.

TIP:

Leave the cookies to cool down completely before lifting them off the sheet, as they will still be very soft after baking. Cookies keep best in a tin, but even then they never stay around very long.

CREAM PUFFS
WITH CHERRY FILLING

Makes 12 small cream puffs

Time: 25 mins prep + 30 mins baking

For the cream puffs:

4 tbsp	vegan margarine
1 cup	all-purpose flour
⅓ cup	cornstarch
1	pinch of salt
2 tbsp	soy cream

For the filling:

12oz (350g)	jar sour cherries, drained, liquid reserved
3 tsp	vanilla extract
2 tbsp	cornstarch
1 cup	soy cream, suitable for whipping, well chilled
1 tsp	cream stiffener

1 Preheat the oven to 400°F (200°C). To make the cream puffs, put 1⅛ cups water into a pan with the margarine and bring to a boil. Combine the flour, cornstarch, and salt, then add to the pan, stirring constantly with a wooden spoon. Next, add the soy cream. Cook the mixture for 1–2 minutes, until it forms a smooth and supple ball and a brown coating forms on the base of the pan.

2 Transfer the ball of dough into a piping bag with a star nozzle attached. Pipe 12 spirals onto a baking sheet lined with parchment paper, leaving a gap between each one. Bake in the center of the oven for 30 minutes until golden brown. Do not open the oven during baking.

3 While the cream puffs are baking, prepare the filling. Put the cherries with ½ cup of the reserved marinating juice and the vanilla extract into a pan and simmer briefly. Add some of the cherry juice to the cornstarch and stir until smooth, then add to the cherry mixture. Continue to simmer until the mix has begun to thicken. Remove from the stove top and leave to cool. Whip the cream with the cream stiffener.

4 Remove the cream puffs from the oven, leave to cool, then slice them open with a bread knife. Spread some cherries onto the bottom halves, then add a layer of cream, and, finally, replace the tops.

TIP:
In fall, you can also make a particularly delicious filling using chestnut purée and whipped soy cream.

BERRY CRUMBLE

For a 8½in (22cm) springform pan (12 pieces)

Time: 35 mins prep + 45 mins baking

For the base:

1 cup	spelt flour
1 cup	whole-grain spelt flour
½ cup	fine cane sugar
1 tsp	baking powder
½ tsp	baking soda
½ tsp	salt
¾ tsp	vanilla powder
1½ tbsp	chickpea flour
¼ cup	vanilla soy milk
¼ cup	vanilla soy yogurt
3 tbsp	canola oil

For the filling:

1lb 5oz (600g)	strawberries (or other berries)
1–2 tsp	vanilla extract
2 tbsp	fine cane sugar

For the crumble:

¼ cup	spelt flour
¼ cup	whole-grain spelt flour
½ tsp	baking powder
4 tbsp	fine cane sugar
3 tbsp	vegan margarine
1–2 tsp	vanilla extract
	some vanilla soy milk

Also:

vegan vanilla ice cream or whipped soy cream, to serve

1 To make the base, combine the spelt flour and whole-grain spelt flour in a bowl. Add the cane sugar, baking powder, baking soda, salt, vanilla powder, and chickpea flour and mix everything together thoroughly. In a separate bowl, stir the soy milk, soy yogurt, and canola oil until smooth. Set both mixtures aside.

2 For the filling, trim and then halve or quarter the strawberries, depending on their size. Mix with the vanilla extract and sugar, then set aside.

3 To make the crumble, combine the flours in a bowl. Mix together with the baking powder and the sugar. Work in some margarine using your fingers until the mixture is a crumbly consistency. Add the vanilla extract. If the mixture is too firm, add a bit of soy milk.

4 Preheat the oven to 350°F (180°C). Line the springform pan with parchment paper. Combine the dry and liquid ingredient mixtures for the base until you have a smooth dough. Put three-quarters of the dough into the pan and smooth it out, then spread the berries over the top and press down gently. Spread the remaining dough mix over the top and smooth it out again. Scatter the crumble over the top.

5 Bake the crumble cake in the center of the oven for 40–45 minutes, until a skewer inserted in the cake comes out clean. Remove the pan from the oven and serve the crumble while still warm with vegan vanilla ice cream or chilled soy cream.

MINI PEANUT AND COCONUT CAKES
WITH CARAMEL

Makes 8 mini cakes

Time: 35 mins prep + 50 mins baking + chilling

For the mini cakes:

1¾ cups	all-purpose flour
1 cup	fine cane sugar
1 tsp	vanilla powder
½ tsp	ground cinnamon
½ tsp	grated nutmeg
½ tsp	ground ginger
1 tsp	baking powder
1 tsp	baking soda
1 tsp	salt
3	very ripe bananas
1⅛ cups	coconut milk
½ cup	canola oil
1 tbsp	cider vinegar

For the peanut frosting:

18 tbsp	soft vegan margarine
½ cup	smooth peanut butter
2 cups	powdered sugar

Also:

2¾oz (80g)	peanuts
	coconut flakes
	vegan caramel sauce (store-bought)

1 Preheat the oven to 325°F (160°C). For the mini cakes, combine the flour, cane sugar, vanilla powder, cinnamon, nutmeg, ginger, baking powder, baking soda, and salt in a bowl. Peel the bananas and mash them to a purée with a fork. In a separate bowl, whisk the coconut milk and canola oil, add the cider vinegar, and stir in the mashed bananas. Quickly stir the liquid ingredients into the dry ingredients until you have a smooth mixture, but take care not to stir too vigorously.

2 Line a 9½in (24cm) springform pan with parchment paper, then transfer the mixture into the pan and smooth it out. Bake in the center of the oven for 45–50 minutes, until a skewer inserted in the cake comes out clean. Remove from the oven and leave to cool completely. Slice the cake in half horizontally and use a glass (about 2¾in/7cm in diameter) to stamp out 16 little round cake bases.

3 For the peanut frosting, use an electric mixer on the highest setting to beat the margarine until creamy, then stir in the peanut butter. Sift over the powdered sugar and, with the mixer on its lowest setting, carefully combine everything. If the frosting is too soft, simply chill it briefly.

4 Transfer the frosting into a piping bag with a round nozzle attached. Pipe blobs of the frosting mixture onto half of the little bases, then carefully put the remaining cake sections on top, and finish with more generous dollops of frosting. Leave to chill. Toast the peanuts and coconut flakes in a dry pan, leave to cool, then scatter over the mini cakes. Drizzle over some caramel sauce and chill the cakes until you are ready to serve.

CAKES, ETC.

Classic, mouth-watering, fruity: Essential recipes for quick, stress-free baking; exquisite coffee morning treats; and feel-good comfort food.

"BUTTER" CAKE

For a 12 × 15½in (30 × 40cm) baking sheet

Time: 20 mins prep + 35 mins baking

For the cake mix:

1½ cups	soy cream, suitable for whipping, well chilled
¾ cup	fine cane sugar
1–2 tsp	vanilla extract
¼ cup	powdered egg substitute, such as Ener-g Egg Replacer
1 cup	all-purpose flour
1 cup	spelt flour with a high gluten content
1	pinch of salt
1 tsp	baking powder

For the topping:

12 tbsp	vegan margarine
¾ cup	fine cane sugar
1–2 tsp	vanilla extract
6 tbsp	soy milk
10oz (300g)	sliced almonds

Also:

vegan margarine, for greasing the baking sheet

1 Preheat the oven to 400°F (200°C). For the cake mix, use a balloon whisk to combine the soy cream, sugar, vanilla extract, and egg substitute until you have a smooth consistency. In a separate bowl, combine the flours, salt, and baking powder. Beat both mixtures together until light and creamy. Spread the mixture over a well-greased baking sheet and bake in the center of the oven for 10 minutes.

2 Meanwhile, for the topping, cream the margarine with the sugar and vanilla extract. Mix in the soy milk and almonds, then spread the sugar and almond mixture evenly over the prebaked base. Cook the cake for a further 20–25 minutes, until the topping is golden brown. Remove from the oven, leave to cool, and cut into 16 pieces.

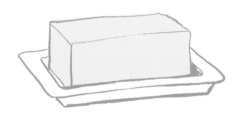

And presto—it's ready! Enjoy this easy-to-make sponge cake with an attractive striped appearance.

QUICK MARBLE CAKE

For a 12in (30cm) long loaf pan

For the pale cake mix:

1¾ cups	all-purpose flour, plus extra for dusting
½ cup	fine cane sugar
1 tsp	baking soda
1¼ cups	soy milk
	grated zest of
1	organic lemon
⅔ cup	corn oil
2–3 tsp	vanilla extract

For the dark cake mix:

1¾ cups	all-purpose flour
½ cup	fine cane sugar
1 tsp	baking soda
¼ cup	vegan cocoa powder
⅔ cup	corn oil
1½ cups	soy milk
2–3 tsp	vanilla extract

Also:

vegan margarine, for greasing the pan

Time: 25 mins prep + 1 hr baking + 15 mins cooling

1 Carefully grease a large loaf pan and dust with flour. To make the pale cake mix, combine the flour, sugar, and baking soda in a bowl. In a separate bowl, whisk the soy milk, lemon zest, and corn oil; add the vanilla extract; and fold these into the dry ingredients. Take care not to stir too vigorously.

2 Preheat the oven to 350°F (180°C). For the dark cake mix, combine the flour, sugar, baking soda, and cocoa powder. In a separate bowl, whisk the corn oil and soy milk, add the vanilla extract, and fold these into the dry ingredients.

3 Put 3 tablespoons of the pale mix into the center of the pan, then add 3 tablespoons of the dark mix on top; continue in this manner until all the cake mix has been used up. Bake the cake in the center of the oven for 50–60 minutes, until a skewer inserted in the cake comes out clean. Leave the cake in the pan and put it on a wire rack to cool for about 15 minutes before turning it out of the pan.

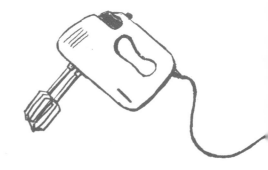

A bread or a cake? Who cares! It's fun to make; healthy; and tastes great plain, with a dollop of soy cream, or with almond butter spread on it.

DELICIOUS
ALMOND BUTTER WHOLE-GRAIN BREAD

For a 11in (28cm) long loaf pan

2½ cups	whole-wheat flour, plus extra for dusting
1 cup + 2 tbsp	fine cane sugar
1	pinch of salt
1	pinch of ground cinnamon
7oz (200g)	ground almonds
1½ tsp	baking soda
1½ tsp	baking powder
¼ cup	soy milk
1 tbsp	cider vinegar
2–3 tsp	vanilla extract
¼ cup	almond milk
¼ cup	canola oil
5 tbsp	almond butter
1	grated zest of small organic lemon
1⅛ cups	carbonated mineral water
	vegan margarine, for greasing the pan

Time: 20 mins prep + 50 mins baking + 10 mins cooling

1 Preheat the oven to 350°F (180°C). Combine the flour, sugar, salt, cinnamon, almonds, baking soda, and baking powder in a bowl. In a separate bowl, whisk the soy milk with the cider vinegar, add the vanilla extract, and leave to thicken for 5 minutes. Stir in the almond milk, canola oil, almond butter, and lemon zest until smooth. Quickly combine the liquid and dry ingredients with a large spoon. Slowly add the mineral water and stir the mix again (not too vigorously) with the spoon until smooth.

2 Grease a loaf pan with margarine and dust with flour. Transfer the mixture to the pan, smooth the surface, and bake in the center of the oven for about 50 minutes, until a skewer inserted in the bread comes out clean.

3 Remove from the oven and leave the bread to cool in the pan for about 10 minutes. Use a knife to gently loosen the loaf around the edges, knock it out of the pan, and leave to cool completely on a wire rack.

TIP:

Transform the bread into more of a cake by topping it with an almond butter and dark chocolate glaze. To do this, spread the bread with almond butter and leave to dry a little. Melt 5½oz (150g) vegan chocolate with 1 tbsp coconut oil and spread this over the almond butter layer. Optionally, toast a handful of sliced almonds in a dry pan and scatter over top.

A crust with a hint of coffee, a delicious vanilla yogurt filling,
and a delicate crumble makes this cake pretty hard to resist.

MARBLED CHOCOLATE CHEESECAKE

For a 8½in (22cm) springform pan

Time: 35 mins prep + 1 hr chilling + 45 mins baking

For the base:

1⅓ cups	all-purpose flour
½ cup	fine cane sugar
2 tsp	baking powder
2 tbsp	cornstarch
¼ cup	vegan cocoa powder
1 tbsp	instant coffee granules, finely ground
1	pinch of salt
9 tbsp	vegan margarine
1–2 tsp	vanilla extract

For the filling:

¼ cup	cornstarch
5 tbsp	vanilla soy milk
1lb 2oz (500g)	vanilla soy yogurt
½ cup	fine cane sugar
1–2 tsp	vanilla extract
1	juice and zest of organic lemon
9 tbsp	vegan margarine

1 For the base, combine the flour, sugar, baking powder, cornstarch, cocoa powder, instant coffee, and salt in a bowl. Add the margarine in little blobs and work it in with your fingers, then add the vanilla extract. If the pastry is too firm, add a few drops of water. Wrap the pastry in plastic wrap and chill for 1 hour in the refrigerator.

2 Preheat the oven to 325°F (160°C) and line the springform pan with parchment paper. Thinly cover the base of the pan with three quarters of the pastry—press it down slightly and bring up the sides so it stands about 1½in (4cm) high. Prick the pastry with a fork and chill it again.

3 To make the filling, stir together the cornstarch and soy milk with a balloon whisk until smooth. Stir in the soy yogurt, sugar, vanilla extract, and lemon juice and zest. In a small pan, melt the margarine over low heat and, when it is lukewarm (not hot), combine it with the soy and sugar cream. Spread the mixture smoothly over the pastry. From the remaining pastry, use your fingers to pull off little crumble pieces and distribute these over the filling mixture.

4 Bake in the center of the oven for 45 minutes, until firm on the outside and slightly jiggly in the middle. Remove the pan from the oven and leave to cool completely.

TIP:

For a really lavish cake, double the ingredients for the topping and use a larger springform (8 or 10½in/ 24 or 26cm in diameter). Bake for about 1 hour.

DANUBE WAVE CAKES

For a 12 × 15½in (30 × 40cm) baking sheet

Time: 35 mins prep + 30 mins baking

For the cake mix:

18 tbsp	soft vegan margarine
1–2 tsp	vanilla extract
1 cup + 2 tbsp	fine cane sugar
3¾ cups	all-purpose flour
1 tsp	baking powder
¼ cup	soy flour
1¼ cups	soy milk
¼ cup	vegan cocoa powder
1½lb (675g)	sour cherries, pitted and drained

For the cream:

3¼ cups	vanilla soy milk
2¾oz (80g)	vanilla instant custard powder
¼ cup	fine cane sugar
18 tbsp	soft vegan margarine

Also:

7oz (200g)	vegan dark chocolate

1 To make the cake, use an electric mixer to cream the margarine with the vanilla extract and sugar. In a separate bowl, combine the flour, baking powder, and soy flour, then fold this into the margarine and sugar mixture. Finally, stir in the soy milk.

2 Preheat the oven to 400°F (200°C). Spread half the mixture over a baking sheet lined with parchment paper. Fold the cocoa powder into the remaining mixture and spread this over the pale cake mix. Draw a fork through both mixtures to create a slightly marbled effect. Scatter the sour cherries evenly over the cake, pressing them down slightly. Bake the cake in the center of the oven for 25–30 minutes. Remove and leave to cool completely.

3 Meanwhile, for the cream, take a few tablespoons of the soy milk and mix this with the custard powder, then stir in the sugar. Bring the remaining soy milk to a boil over medium heat. Remove the pan from the stove top, stir in the custard paste, then bring everything back to a boil, stirring constantly. Leave the custard to cool to room temperature.

4 Beat the margarine until it is fluffy, then stir in the custard a spoonful at a time. Spread this creamy mixture over the cake and smooth the surface. Melt the dark chocolate in a double boiler, let it cool slightly, and quickly spread it over the creamy layer. Keep the cake chilled until ready to serve, then cut into 12 pieces.

The classic German "bee sting cake" consists of a light yeast dough,
a fine custard and cream filling, and a sweet layer of almonds—
there is nothing else quite like it.

BEE STING CAKE

For a 12 × 15½in (30 × 40cm) baking sheet **Time: 30 mins prep + 45 mins proofing + 30 mins baking**

For the base:

5¼ cups	spelt flour with a high gluten content, plus extra to work with
1½ tsp	dried yeast
1	pinch of salt
½ cup	fine cane sugar
7 tbsp	vegan margarine
¾ cup	soy milk

For the topping:

11 tbsp	vegan margarine
⅔ cup	fine cane sugar
7oz (200g)	sliced almonds

For the filling:

1¼ cups	rice cream, suitable for whipping, well chilled
4 cups	vanilla soy milk
4½oz (125g)	instant custard powder
½	seeds scraped from vanilla bean
⅓ cup	fine cane sugar
1	pinch of salt
2 tbsp	vegan margarine

1 To make the base, combine the flour, yeast, salt, and sugar in a bowl. Melt the margarine in a small pan and stir it into the dry ingredients. Heat the soy milk and ¾ cup water over low heat, then add these to the mix. Knead everything together until you have a smooth, supple dough. Cover the dough and leave to proof in a warm place for about 45 minutes.

2 Preheat the oven to 350°F (180°C). Roll out the dough and place it on a baking sheet lined with parchment paper.

3 To make the topping, heat the margarine with the sugar in a pan over medium heat, stirring constantly until melted, then mix in the sliced almonds. Spread the mixture evenly over the base using a dough scraper. Bake in the center of the oven for 25–30 minutes. Remove from the oven and allow it to cool.

4 Meanwhile, make the filling by beating the rice cream, using an electric mixer on its highest setting, and leave to chill. Take ¾ cup of the soy milk and stir together with the custard powder until smooth. Put the remaining soy milk and the vanilla seeds, sugar, and salt into a pan and bring to a boil over medium heat. Remove the pan from the stove top and stir in the custard paste made earlier. Bring the mixture back to a boil, stirring constantly. Remove the pan from the stove top once again and stir in the margarine. Leave the custard to cool, then fold in the rice cream.

5 Once the base is cool, cut it into 12 pieces. Slice each piece in half horizontally and fill with the cream.

CARROT CAKE

WITH WHITE CHOCOLATE AND CREAM CHEESE ICING

Here, the carrots go beautifully with the sweet white chocolate and cream cheese in the icing. Pistachios add the perfect finishing touch to the whole combination.

For a 9½in (24cm) springform pan

Time: 35 mins prep + 65 mins baking

For the cake:

2¾ cups	all-purpose flour
2 tsp	baking soda
1½ cups	fine cane sugar
1	seeds scraped from vanilla bean
1 tsp	salt
2 tsp	(slightly heaped) ground cinnamon
2 tsp	baking powder
14oz (400g)	soy yogurt
¾ cup	corn oil
14oz (400g)	carrots, very finely grated

For the icing:

3½oz (100g)	vegan white chocolate
6 tbsp	soft vegan margarine
4½oz (125g)	vegan cream cheese
6 tbsp	powdered sugar
1	grated zest of organic lemon

Also:

3½oz (100g)	pistachios, chopped

1 Preheat the oven to 350°F (180°C). To make the cake, combine the flour, baking soda, cane sugar, vanilla seeds, salt, and cinnamon in a medium-sized bowl. Sift in the baking powder and stir everything together again.

2 In a separate larger bowl, use a balloon whisk to mix the soy yogurt and corn oil, then vigorously stir in the grated carrot using a spoon. Add the dry ingredients in two stages, using a large spoon to mix everything to an even consistency and only stirring as much as required to combine the carrot mixture with the flour.

3 Line the springform pan with parchment paper. Transfer the cake mixture into the pan and smooth the surface. Bake the cake in the center of the oven for 65 minutes. Remove and leave to cool completely.

4 To make the icing, melt the white chocolate in a double boiler, then leave to cool to room temperature. Use an electric mixer on its highest setting to beat the margarine and the cream cheese. Sift over the powdered sugar and mix this in along with the lemon zest, using the mixer on a medium setting. Gradually pour in the chocolate, incorporating it into the mixture with the mixer on a low setting. The result should be a smooth, creamy, soft icing, which will firm up in the refrigerator. Spread the icing over the carrot cake and smooth the surface. Scatter with the chopped pistachios and chill the carrot cake until ready to serve.

This gluten-free carrot cake tart contains no processed sugar and is made from raw ingredients. The base is sweetened purely using dates, and the tart is finished off with a wonderfully creamy macadamia and vanilla filling.

CARROT CAKE TART

WITH MACADAMIA AND VANILLA CREAM

RAW & GLUTEN-FREE

For a 8in (20cm) springform pan (12 pieces)

Time: 20 mins prep + 12 hrs soaking + 2 hrs chilling

For the cream filling:

4½oz (125g)	macadamia nuts
⅓ cup	coconut oil
3 tbsp	maple syrup
	seeds scraped from
1	vanilla bean
	juice of
½	lemon
1	pinch of salt

For the base:

3	medium carrots
3¼oz (90g)	hazelnuts
5oz (140g)	dates, pitted
1¼oz (40g)	fine coconut flakes
1	pinch of salt
dash	grated nutmeg
1 tsp	ground cinnamon

Also:

12	macadamia nuts, for decorating

1 For the cream filling, first soak the macadamia nuts overnight in water.

2 For the base, peel and finely grate the carrots. Use a food processor to finely chop the hazelnuts and dates. Add the coconut flakes, salt, nutmeg, and cinnamon and process everything until you have a smooth paste. Mix in the grated carrot. Transfer the mixture to a springform pan lined with parchment paper, press the mixture down slightly, and use your fingers to press up the sides until you have an edge that is about ¾in (2cm) high. Refrigerate.

3 Meanwhile, to make the cream filling, melt the coconut oil in a small pan over low heat. Drain the macadamia nuts and blend them in a food processor with the coconut oil, maple syrup, vanilla seeds, lemon juice, salt, and ¼ cup water until you have a delicious, smooth cream. Spread the cream over the base, smooth the surface, and chill the cake in the refrigerator for at least 2 hours. Garnish with macadamia nuts.

This sweet flower always creates a bit of a sensation at the breakfast table or at a cookout with friends.

SWEET RASPBERRY FLOWER

For a 12in (30cm) springform pan (16 pieces)

For the dough:

2¼ tsp	dried yeast
4 tbsp	vegan margarine
4¼ cups	spelt flour, plus extra for dusting
½ cup	fine cane sugar
2 tsp	salt

For the filling:

10oz (300g)	raspberries (frozen)
2 tbsp	fine cane sugar
1¾oz (50g)	sliced almonds
2	mint leaves

Time: 35 mins prep + 55 mins proofing + 30 mins baking

1 To make the dough, put 1 cup + 2 tablespoons lukewarm water into a bowl and add the yeast. Cover and leave to proof at room temperature for about 10 minutes, then use a balloon whisk to mix to a smooth consistency. Melt the margarine in a small pan over low heat. Combine the flour, sugar, and salt in a bowl.

2 Add the water and yeast mixture to the dry ingredients along with the margarine, and knead everything to create a smooth dough. Cover and leave to proof in a warm place until it has doubled in size.

3 Meanwhile, for the filling, heat the raspberries with the sugar over low heat. Purée, leave to cool briefly, then fold in the almonds. Finely chop the mint leaves and add these, too.

4 Knead the dough through once more and divide into 3 equal-sized portions. Roll these out on a floured work surface to create roughly ½in (1cm) thick disks with a diameter of about 12in (30cm). Place the first disk into the springform pan, cover it with half the raspberry and almond mixture, then place the second disk on top and cover with the remaining raspberry and almond mixture. Place the third disk of dough on top to form the final layer—this does not get a raspberry topping.

5 Preheat the oven to 350°F (180°C). Use a glass (about ¾in/8cm in diameter) to create an indentation in the center of the dough disk. Cut the dough just as far as this glass indentation to create 16 equal sections. Now take hold of each piece (grasping the top and bottom layers together) and twist it 3 times. Finally, fold over the outer edges of 2 adjacent pieces, shaping them to be nice and round, and join them together to create a "flower petal." Repeat to create 7 more petals. Bake the flower in the center of the oven for 30 minutes.

BANANA BREAD

For a 11in (28cm) long loaf pan

Time: 20 mins prep + 1 hr baking

For the dough:

2 cups	all-purpose flour, plus extra for dusting
2 tbsp	cornstarch
1 heaped tsp	baking powder
1¼ tsp	baking soda
½ tsp	salt
1 cup + 2 tbsp	fine cane sugar
1 tsp	vanilla powder
½ tsp	ground cinnamon
¼ tsp	grated nutmeg
½ cup	soy milk
⅓ cup	canola oil
7oz (200g)	vegan sour cream (or soy yogurt with a squeeze of lemon)
4	medium, very ripe bananas

Also:

vegan margarine, for greasing the pan
powdered sugar, for dusting

1 Preheat the oven to 350°F (180°C). In a large bowl, combine the flour, cornstarch, baking powder, baking soda, salt, cane sugar, vanilla powder, cinnamon, and nutmeg.

2 In a separate bowl, stir the soy milk with the canola oil and sour cream until smooth. Peel the bananas and mash well with a fork until you have a creamy mixture with an even consistency. Stir the banana purée into the soy milk mixture. Quickly stir together the liquid and dry ingredients with a spoon until there are no lumps in the mix.

3 Grease a loaf pan with margarine and dust with flour. Transfer the mixture to the pan, smooth the surface, and bake the bread in the center of the oven for 50–60 minutes, until a skewer inserted in the bread comes out clean.

TIP:

Banana bread tastes great plain or spread with some vegan margarine. To decorate, you can also make an icing by stirring together some powdered sugar and banana juice. Spread this on top of the bread and scatter over some chopped banana chips to decorate.

Chocolate lovers and fruit fans both get their money's worth here. This chocolate cake can be made with almost any type of fruit or berries. Enveloped in a delicate chocolate glaze and topped with toasted almonds, this is a truly special creation.

CHOCOLATEY FRUIT CAKE

For a 9 × 9in (23 × 23cm) baking pan

Time: 30 mins prep + 40 mins baking

For the cake:

1lb 2oz (500g)	seasonal fruit
2 cups	soy milk
3 tsp	cider vinegar
¾ cup	fine cane sugar
1–2 tsp	vanilla extract
2 cups	whole-grain spelt flour
¼ cup	vegan cocoa powder, sifted
1½ tsp	baking soda
1 tsp	baking powder
½ tsp	salt
½ cup	sunflower oil

Also:

5½oz (150g)	vegan dark chocolate
1 tbsp	coconut oil
	sliced almonds, for scattering

1 Preheat the oven to 350°F (180°C). To make the cake, first chop the fruit into pieces. In a bowl, whisk the soy milk with the cider vinegar and leave to thicken for 5 minutes. Stir in the sugar and vanilla extract with a balloon whisk. In a separate bowl, combine the flour, cocoa powder, baking soda, baking powder, and salt. Fold the dry ingredients into the liquid mixture and combine until you have a smooth consistency. Next, stir in the sunflower oil and combine well with the mixture. Finally fold in the fruit.

2 Transfer the mixture to a pan lined with parchment paper, smooth the surface, and bake in the center of the oven for about 40 minutes, until a skewer inserted in the cake comes out clean. Remove and leave to cool completely.

3 Melt the chocolate with the coconut oil in a double boiler, stir until smooth, and cover the cake all over. Carefully toast the sliced almonds in a dry pan and scatter them over the still-molten chocolate. Slice the cake into about 16 pieces to serve.

TIP:

It is important to wash and chop the fresh fruit at the start, because the mix shouldn't be left to stand for too long. If you use canned or frozen fruit, this will need to be thoroughly drained or squeezed so the cake doesn't get soggy. If necessary, reduce the quantity of fruit slightly.

Juicy pears on a pale base, covered with a delicate marzipan crumble—a really luxurious cake!

PEAR CAKE
WITH MARZIPAN CRUMBLE

For a 12 × 15½in (30 × 40cm) baking sheet

Time: 40 mins prep + 1 hr proofing + 50 mins baking

For the filling:

3lb 3oz (1.5kg)	pears
¼ cup	fine cane sugar
2–3 tsp	vanilla extract

For the base:

2¾ cups	spelt flour
½ cup	fine cane sugar
1	pinch of salt
¾ cup	soy milk
1–2 tsp	vanilla extract
2¼ tsp	dried yeast
4 tbsp	vegan margarine

For the marzipan crumble:

1¼ cups	spelt flour
3 tbsp	cane sugar
7 tbsp	vegan margarine
7oz (200g)	marzipan
1–2 tsp	vanilla extract

1 Prepare the filling by peeling and quartering the pears, then remove the cores and chop the pears into cubes. Place the fruit in a pan, add the sugar and vanilla extract, and cook for 8–10 minutes over medium heat initially, then reduce to low heat. Leave to cool.

2 For the base, combine the flour, sugar, and salt in a bowl. Gently heat the soy milk in a small pan over low heat and add the vanilla extract. Pour this into a separate bowl, sprinkle the yeast over the milk, and leave to stand for about 10 minutes.

3 In the meantime, add blobs of the margarine to the flour mixture and quickly work them in until the flour has completely absorbed the fat. Stir the milk and yeast mixture until smooth, then knead this in; the yeast dough should be nice and smooth. Cover and leave to proof in a warm place for about 30 minutes.

4 Line a baking sheet with parchment paper and roll the dough out on it, creating a slight rim around the edge. Leave the dough to proof for about 20 minutes.

5 Preheat the oven to 350°F (180°C). To make the crumble, mix the flour with the sugar. Add the margarine and marzipan in little pieces, working them in with your fingers to create a crumbly texture. Add the vanilla extract. Spread the pear filling evenly over the base. Scatter the crumble over the filling and bake the cake in the center of the oven for 40–50 minutes. Remove from the oven and leave to cool. Cut into 12 pieces.

TIP:

Try sprinkling with powdered sugar to serve. This cake tastes delicious served warm with some vegan vanilla ice cream.

PEAR JUICE TART
WITH CINNAMON CREAM

For a 10½in (26cm) springform pan (12 pieces)

Time: 40 mins prep + 1 hr chilling + 1 hr baking

For the base:

1¾ cups	all-purpose flour
½ cup	fine cane sugar
1 tsp	baking powder
10 tbsp	vegan margarine
1–2 tsp	vanilla extract

For the filling:

1¾lb (800g)	pears
3½ cups	pear juice
⅔ cup	cornstarch
6 tbsp	fine cane sugar
1–2 tsp	vanilla extract

Also:

1 cup	soy cream, suitable for whipping, well chilled
	ground cinnamon, for dusting

1 To make the base, combine the flour, sugar, and baking powder in a bowl. Work in the margarine using your fingers, add the vanilla extract, and bring everything together to create a smooth pie dough. Line a springform pan with parchment paper. Put the pastry into the pan, pressing it down and smoothing it out with a tablespoon. Create a rim of 2¾in (7cm) up the sides. Prick the base with a fork and leave to chill for 1 hour.

2 Meanwhile, to make the filling, peel and quarter the pears, remove the cores, and dice the pears finely. Put the pear juice into a pan. In a bowl, mix the cornstarch with the sugar, add a bit of the pear juice and vanilla extract, and stir until the mixture is smooth and there are no visible lumps.

3 Preheat the oven to 350°F (180°C). Bring the pear juice to a boil over medium heat, remove the pan from the stove top, and stir in the cornstarch mixture. Bring the mixture back to a boil, stirring constantly, then quickly fold in the diced pear. Pour over the crust base and bake the tart in the center of the oven for 1 hour. Remove and leave to cool completely in the pan.

4 Whip the soy cream and then chill until ready to serve. Cut the tart into 12 pieces, put a generous blob of cream on each portion, and dust with plenty of cinnamon.

TIP:

This recipe also tastes fantastic made with apples and apple juice. Drizzle the diced fruit with lemon juice to prevent it from going brown.

APRICOT STRUDEL TART
WITH ALMONDS AND SESAME SEEDS

For a 9½in (24cm) springform pan (12–14 pieces)

Time: 40 mins prep + 35 mins baking

For the strudel tart:

1	pack phyllo pastry (10 sheets, measuring 12 × 12in/30 × 30cm)
10	apricots
14oz (400g)	apples
4 tbsp	vegan margarine
1 cup	whole-wheat breadcrumbs
2 tbsp	cane sugar
1–2 tsp	vanilla extract
1¾oz (50g)	chopped almonds
scant 1oz (25g)	sesame seeds
½ cup	ground almonds
1 tsp	ground cinnamon
½ tsp	ground cardamom
1	pinch of ground ginger
5 tbsp	maple syrup

Also:

scant 1oz (25g)	sesame seeds
scant 1oz (25g)	sliced almonds
3 tbsp	maple syrup

1 Remove the phyllo pastry from the refrigerator 10 minutes before preparation.

2 Preheat the oven to 350°F (180°C). Halve, pit, and dice the apricots. Peel, core, and finely dice the apples. Melt 2 tbsp margarine in a pan over medium heat and toast the breadcrumbs in the fat. Stir in the sugar and vanilla extract. Briefly cook the chopped almonds with the sesame seeds in a dry pan until pale brown. Combine these with the ground almonds. Mix the cinnamon with the cardamom and ginger. Melt the remaining margarine.

3 Place 2 sheets of phyllo on top of each other, brush with a thin layer of margarine, top with one-fifth each of the fruit, the breadcrumbs, the almond and sesame seed mixture, and the spices. As you work, leave a gap of about 1½in (3cm) free around the edges. Finally, drizzle with 1 tablespoon maple syrup. Fold in the sides and roll up the strudel lengthwise. Repeat four more times with the remaining ingredients.

4 Line a springform pan with parchment paper and place the strudels inside, one beside the other in a spiral formation. (It doesn't matter if the phyllo tears a bit at the top.) Finally, brush the strudel tart with margarine.

5 Toast the sesame seeds and sliced almonds in a dry pan and scatter them over the strudel tart. Drizzle with maple syrup, and bake in the center of the oven for 35 minutes. Remove and leave to cool completely.

TIP:

Optionally, take 2 cups of well-chilled soy cream, suitable for whipping, add 2 tsp of cream stiffener and 2 tsp ground vanilla, then beat with an electric mixer for 3 minutes until stiff. Spread over the tart.

Fruity on the bottom, fluffy on the top: this moist poppy seed and redcurrant cake is topped with a vegan version of fluffy meringue. This cake looks absolutely stunning.

POPPY SEED AND REDCURRANT CAKE
WITH A MERINGUE TOPPING

For a 12 × 15½in (30 × 40cm) baking sheet

Time: 40 mins prep + 40 mins baking

For the cake:

2⅓ cups	whole-wheat flour
1 tbsp	cornstarch
1 tsp	(slightly heaped) baking powder
1 tsp	(slightly heaped) baking soda
2¼oz (70g)	ground poppy seeds
1 cup	fine cane sugar
2 tsp	vanilla powder
1 cup + 2 tbsp	soy milk
1 tbsp	cider vinegar
½ cup	canola oil
12oz (350g)	redcurrants

For the meringue topping:

2 tbsp	powdered egg substitute, such as Ener-g Egg Replacer
1 cup + 2 tbsp	fine cane sugar
1 tbsp	agar-agar
1	generous splash rum
	some powdered sugar, to dust

1 Preheat the oven to 350°F (180°C). To make the cake, combine the dry ingredients in a large bowl. In a separate bowl, whisk the soy milk with the cider vinegar and leave to thicken for 5 minutes. Add the canola oil and ⅔ cup water and whisk everything together. Stir the liquid mixture into the dry ingredients—a couple of lumps here and there won't matter.

2 Line a high-sided baking sheet with parchment paper. Smooth the cake mixture out over the sheet. Scatter the redcurrants over and press them down slightly. Bake the cake in the center of the oven for 30–40 minutes, until a skewer inserted in the cake comes out clean. Remove and leave to cool completely.

3 Preheat the oven to 475°F (240°C) with the broiler setting enabled. To make the meringue, put the egg substitute and 1¼ cups water into a container and beat with an electric mixer on its highest setting for 5 minutes, then sprinkle in ⅔ cup of the sugar and continue to beat.

4 In a pan, bring ¾ cup water to a boil with the remaining ½ cup sugar and the agar-agar, stirring constantly, then add the rum. As soon as the sugar has dissolved, stir this quickly into the meringue mixture.

5 Spread the mixture over the cake, shaping it into waves and dusting with powdered sugar. Bake for 1–2 minutes under the broiler until the topping has browned slightly. Remove from the oven, leave to cool, and refrigerate. To serve, slice into 12 pieces.

TIP:
Keep a very close eye on the cake while it's under the broiler—meringue burns very easily! For a less sweet version, simply halve the meringue ingredients.

This fruity treat is topped with an exquisite creamy layer of icing and delicate flowers. It looks impressive, but it is super quick to make.

RASPBERRY AND GOOSEBERRY CAKE

For a 9 × 9in (23 × 23cm) square springform pan

Time: 40 mins prep + 40 mins baking

For the cake:

3 tbsp	canola oil
¾ cup	chickpea flour
1⅓ cups	powdered sugar
1⅓ cups	all-purpose flour
2 tsp	baking powder
1 tsp	baking soda
1 tsp	vanilla powder
1	pinch of salt
2 tsp	cider vinegar
⅓ cup	soy milk
5½oz (150g)	raspberries
3½oz (100g)	gooseberries

For the icing:

⅓ cup	cornstarch
½ tsp	ground vanilla
1 cup + 2 tbsp	raspberry juice (online)
10 tbsp	soft vegan margarine
⅓ cup	powdered sugar
	edible flowers, such as pink and white daisies, to decorate (optional)

1 Preheat the oven to 350°F (180°C). Line a square springform pan with parchment paper. To make the cake, whisk the canola oil with ⅔ cup water in a bowl, then use an electric mixer to beat in the chickpea flour. Add the powdered sugar with the mixer on its highest setting.

2 In a separate bowl, combine the all-purpose flour, baking powder, baking soda, vanilla powder, and salt. Stir this into the chickpea mix by the spoonful, then quickly combine everything with the spoon until smooth.

3 Stir the cider vinegar into the soy milk, leave to thicken for about 5 minutes, stir it all through again, then fold into the cake mix using a spoon. Transfer the mixture into the pan and smooth the surface. Mix the berries and scatter them over the cake, pressing down slightly. Bake in the center of the oven for about 40 minutes, until a skewer inserted in the cake comes out clean. Remove and leave to cool completely.

4 To make the icing, combine the cornstarch with the vanilla in a pan. Stir in the raspberry juice until smooth and bring to a boil over medium heat, stirring constantly. As soon as the mixture has thickened, remove the pan from the heat and allow the mixture to cool to room temperature, stirring occasionally.

5 Use an electric mixer on its highest setting to cream the margarine in a bowl. Sift over the powdered sugar and mix it in with the mixer on a medium setting. Then fold the vanilla and raspberry cream into the margarine and sugar mixture, one spoonful at a time. Stir it all together until smooth, then spread over the cake. If desired, decorate the cake with edible flowers before slicing into 12 pieces.

TIP:

Lots of other seasonal berries will also taste great—you could try combining the raspberries with blackcurrants.

These lovely, cream-filled sandwich cookies are vegan, so they don't just play a supporting role in this "cheesecake"—they are given star billing.

OREO "CHEESECAKE"

For a 9½in (24cm) springform pan (12 pieces)

Time: 35 mins prep + 12 hrs draining + 2 hrs cooling and baking

For the filling:

2¼lb (1kg)	soy yogurt
1	juice and zest of organic lemon
3½ tbsp	canola oil
½ cup	soy milk
½ cup	cornstarch
¾ cup	fine cane sugar
1	pinch of salt
1 tsp	vanilla powder (or the seeds from vanilla bean)
1	

For the base:

4 tbsp	vegan margarine
16	Oreo cookies, plus
4	cookies reserved for decoration

1 Line a sieve with a clean kitchen towel and place it over a large bowl. Pour in the soy yogurt and leave to drain overnight. The following day, squeeze out any excess water from the yogurt.

2 To make the base, melt the margarine in a pan over low heat. Use a food processor to pulse the Oreo cookies to make crumbs. Gradually add the margarine and pulse until everything is combined. Line a springform pan with parchment paper. Cover the base with a thin layer of the cookie mixture, press it down slightly with a spoon, and smooth the surface. Leave to chill in the refrigerator for at least 1 hour.

3 Preheat the oven to 350°F (180°C). To make the filling, put the soy yogurt into a bowl and stir in the lemon juice, lemon zest, and canola oil until smooth. In a separate bowl, stir the soy milk and cornstarch until smooth, then mix in the sugar, salt, and vanilla powder. Finally, stir everything into the soy yogurt and lemon mixture until you have a smooth and creamy consistency. Spread this mixture over the cookie base.

4 Carefully twist apart the 2 layers of the Oreo cookies you saved for decoration and arrange them on the cheesecake, creamy side down, pressing them slightly into the mixture. Bake in the center of the oven for 50–60 minutes. Remove from the oven, leave to cool slightly, then transfer to the refrigerator to cool completely.

RAW & GLUTEN-FREE

"CHEESECAKE" WITH MANGO CREAM

For a 11in (28cm) springform pan (12–14 pieces)

Time: 20 mins prep + 3 hrs chilling

For the base:

2 tbsp	coconut oil
7oz (200g)	cashew nuts
5½oz (150g)	macadamia nuts
3½oz (100g)	fine coconut flakes
1 tbsp	lemon juice
1 tsp	grated organic lemon zest
1 tbsp	agave syrup
1	pinch of salt

For the filling:

10 tbsp	coconut oil
1lb 10oz (50g)	cashew nuts
⅔ cup	lemon juice
⅓ cup	agave syrup
½	seeds scraped from vanilla bean

For the mango cream:

10oz (300g)	mango chips, plus extra for decorating (from an organic or health food store)
1 tbsp	psyllium husks
2 tbsp	agave syrup
1 tbsp	lemon juice

1 Melt the coconut oil for both the base and the filling in a small pan over low heat. To make the base, finely grind the cashew and macadamia nuts in a food processor. Add 2 tablespoons coconut oil and the remaining base ingredients, plus the salt, and process everything until you have a uniform mixture. Transfer to a springform pan lined with parchment paper, smooth the surface, then chill for 30 minutes.

2 To make the filling, combine the remaining coconut oil with the other ingredients in a food processor on its highest setting until it forms a well-combined, smooth paste. If it is too thick, add a bit of water and mix again. Spread the filling over the base and transfer to the freezer for 30 minutes.

3 In the meantime, make the mango cream by mixing all the ingredients in a food processor on its highest setting until you have a smooth consistency. Spread this quickly over the frozen surface of the cheesecake. (It will set rapidly.) Put the cheesecake in the refrigerator for at least 2 hours and scatter with mango chips before serving.

TIP:

If you are short on time, you can simply put the cheesecake in the freezer for 1 hour before serving.

ALMOND "CHEESECAKE"
WITH BLUEBERRIES

For a 9½in (24cm) springform pan (12–14 pieces)

Time: 45 mins prep + 70 mins baking + at least 1 hr chilling

For the base:

1¾ cups	all-purpose flour
½ tsp	baking powder
⅔ cup	fine cane sugar
10 tbsp	vegan margarine, chilled
1–2 tsp	vanilla extract

For the filling:

12oz (350g)	blanched whole almonds (alternatively, ground almonds)
1lb 2oz (500g)	soy yogurt
¾ cup	fine cane sugar
1–2 tsp	vanilla extract
2	juice and zest of organic lemons
⅔ cup	cornstarch
⅔ cup	almond milk
8 tbsp	coconut oil
9oz (250g)	blueberries

Also:

1 tsp	clear cake glaze, vegan
¼ cup	fine cane sugar

1. To make the base, combine the flour, baking powder, and sugar in a bowl. Add the margarine and vanilla extract and use your fingers to quickly work the ingredients to create a smooth crust texture. Place in a springform pan lined with parchment paper, making sure the pastry comes about 2¾in (7cm) up the sides. Prick the base with a fork and leave to chill.

2. Preheat the oven to 350°F (180°C). For the filling, finely grind the almonds in a food processor on its highest setting. Mix the almonds, soy yogurt, sugar, vanilla extract, and lemon juice and zest and leave to rest briefly. Stir the cornstarch into the almond milk until smooth and add this to the main mixture.

3. Melt the coconut oil in a small pan over low heat, then quickly stir it into the almond and yogurt mixture with a balloon whisk and pour this into your crust base. Bake the cheesecake in the center of the oven for 70 minutes. Remove from the oven and leave to cool for about 1 hour.

4. Top the "cheesecake" with the blueberries. In a saucepan, mix the cake glaze with the sugar and 1 cup + 2 tablespoons cold water, stirring until smooth. Bring briefly to a boil and let it cool slightly while stirring, then carefully distribute it over the blueberries using a spoon. The cheesecake tastes best if the flavors are left to develop overnight.

TIP:

You can also use frozen blueberries instead of fresh. To make sure the filling doesn't get soggy, you should spread 2 tbsp vegan cream stiffener over the surface before you add the berries.

SWISS ROLL
WITH RASPBERRY CREAM

Makes 1 Swiss roll (10–12 pieces)

For the cake mix:

1⅔ cups	all-purpose flour
2 tbsp	cornstarch
1 tsp	baking powder
5½oz (150g)	vanilla soy yogurt
½ cup	soy milk
¼ cup	soy flour
2 tbsp	canola oil
⅔ cup	fine cane sugar, plus extra for sprinkling

For the raspberry cream:

¾ cup	soy cream, suitable for whipping, well chilled
1 tsp	cream stiffener
5½oz (150g)	vanilla soy yogurt
5½oz (150g)	raspberries

Also:

powdered sugar, for dusting

Time: 30 mins prep + 15 mins baking

1 Preheat the oven to 350°F (180°C) and line a baking sheet with parchment paper. To make the cake for the Swiss roll, sift the flour, cornstarch, and baking powder into a large bowl. In a separate bowl, stir together the soy yogurt, soy milk, soy flour, canola oil, and cane sugar until the sugar has dissolved as much as possible. Stir the liquid ingredients into the dry ingredients and spread the mixture over the parchment paper. Bake the cake in the center of the oven for 12–15 minutes.

2 In the meantime, sprinkle sugar over a clean kitchen towel. Turn the cake out onto the towel while it is still hot and carefully pull off the parchment paper. Carefully use the towel to roll up the cake to create a Swiss roll shape, then leave to cool completely.

3 To make the raspberry cream, whip the soy cream using an electric mixer on its highest setting for at least 3 minutes, gradually adding the cream stiffener at the end as you mix. Then stir in the soy yogurt. Carefully fold in the raspberries and leave to chill briefly. Unroll the cake and spread with the raspberry cream, leaving a ¾in (2cm) gap around the edges. Then roll it up again and refrigerate. Serve dusted with powdered sugar.

TIP:

If you prefer a firmer consistency for your cream filling, let the yogurt drain overnight in a sieve lined with a kitchen towel. The resulting "cheese" can be folded into the soy cream as described above.

CAKES AND TARTS

Impressive dishes for guests and parties: exquisite creamy creations to enchant your friends, eye-catching festive treats, and cakes perfect for birthdays.

This edible "molehill" is a sweet mound of cake with a dark base, plenty of cream, and shards of chocolate, and is covered in large crumble pieces.

MOLEHILL CAKE

For a 9½in (24cm) springform pan (12 pieces)

Time: 35 mins prep + 40 mins baking + at least 13 hrs chilling

For the crumble:

2 cups	all-purpose flour
⅔ cup	fine cane sugar
1 tbsp	vegan cocoa powder, sifted
10 tbsp	vegan margarine
1 tsp	vanilla extract

For the base:

1 cup	all-purpose flour
2 tbsp	cornstarch
1 cup	powdered sugar, sifted
1 tbsp	vegan cocoa powder, sifted
1½ tsp	baking powder
½ tsp	vanilla powder
1	pinch of salt
½ cup	soy milk
5 tbsp	canola oil

For the topping:

2 cups	soy cream, suitable for whipping, well chilled
2 tsp	cream stiffener
6	medium bananas
2¾oz (80g)	vegan dark chocolate
3 tbsp	apricot jam

1 Preheat the oven to 350°F (180°C). To make the crumble, combine the flour, cane sugar, and cocoa powder in a bowl. Add the margarine in blobs with the vanilla extract and work into the mix with your fingers to create a rough crumble. Spread the crumble over a baking sheet lined with parchment paper, then bake in the center of the oven for about 20 minutes.

2 For the base, combine the flour, cornstarch, powdered sugar, cocoa powder, baking powder, vanilla powder, and salt in a bowl. In a separate bowl, whisk the soy milk and canola oil. Stir the liquid and dry ingredients together quickly with a large spoon. Line a springform pan with parchment paper, spoon in the mixture, smooth the surface, and bake in the center of the oven for about 20 minutes, until a skewer inserted in it comes out clean. Remove from the oven and leave to cool completely.

3 Meanwhile, for the topping, beat the soy cream with an electric mixer on its highest setting; after about 2 minutes, add the cream stiffener and continue to beat for a further 2–3 minutes. Peel 3 of the bananas, mash them to a pulp with a fork, and fold into the cream. Chop the dark chocolate, fold this into the banana and cream mixture, and transfer to the refrigerator to chill for at least 1 hour.

4 Gently heat the apricot jam in a small pan over low heat and spread it over the base of the cake. Peel the remaining bananas, slice into disks, and place them on the base. Spread the banana cream over the top and return the cake to the fridge to chill for a few minutes. Cover the creamy topping with crumble pieces and leave the cake to firm up in the fridge overnight.

TIP: You can also make the crumble finer and pile up the cream in a dome shape on top of the cake to make it look even more like a molehill.

BANANA CAKE
WITH SOUR CREAM AND CHOCOLATE FROSTING

For a 9½in (24cm) springform pan (12–14 pieces)

Time: 45 mins prep + 1 hr baking + 12 hrs chilling

For the cake:

3¼ cups	all-purpose flour
1 tsp	baking powder
1⅛ cups	fine cane sugar
1 tsp	vanilla powder
2 tbsp	cornstarch
	lemon zest
½ cup	corn oil
½ cup	rice milk
1½ cups	carbonated mineral water

For the frosting:

12oz (350g)	vegan dark chocolate
8 tbsp	vegan margarine
½ tsp	vanilla powder
10oz (300g)	vegan sour cream (at room temperature)
6½ cups	powdered sugar

For the filling and decoration:

5	medium bananas
	rum
	dark and white vegan chocolate, grated (optional)

1 Preheat the oven to 350°F (180°C). For the cake, combine the flour, baking powder, cane sugar, vanilla powder, cornstarch, and lemon zest. Whisk the corn oil with the rice milk and add to the dry ingredients. Slowly stir in the mineral water with a spoon until all the lumps in the mixture are gone.

2 Line a springform pan with parchment paper, put the mixture into the pan, and bake in the center of the oven for about 1 hour. When a skewer inserted in the cake comes out clean, the cake is ready. Leave to cool completely.

3 To make the frosting, break the chocolate into pieces and melt with the margarine in a double boiler. Stir the vanilla powder into the sour cream and fold this into the chocolate mixture. Sift over the powdered sugar and mix it in with an electric mixer. Slice the cake horizontally into 3 layers. Place one of the layers on a cake plate, put a cake ring around it, and spread with a thin layer of the frosting.

4 Peel the bananas for the filling and slice thinly. Distribute half of the slices over the frosting and press down slightly. Place the second cake layer on top and drizzle with rum. Cover with a thin layer of frosting and top with sliced banana. Put the third cake layer on top and likewise drizzle with rum before spreading over the frosting. Run a knife between the edge of the cake and the ring to release it. Cover the sides of the cake with the remaining frosting and decorate the cake with grated chocolate, if using. Ideally, put it in the refrigerator overnight to let the flavors develop.

A cake for special occasions and courageous bakers! A bit of effort is required here, but it is well worth it. Make sure you invite some friends over to eat it, or hold a party as soon as the cake is ready!

NEAPOLITAN WAFER CAKE

For two 9½in (24cm) springform pans (12 pieces)

Time: 45 mins prep + 40 mins baking + at least 12 hrs chilling

For the cake layers:

3½ cups	all-purpose flour
2⅔ cups	ground hazelnuts
1¾ cups	fine cane sugar
2 tbsp	baking powder
1 tsp	ground vanilla
2 cups	vanilla soy milk
1 cup	canola oil

For the filling:

4⅔ cups	soy cream, suitable for whipping, well chilled
4	packs of Neapolitan wafer cookies (each weighing 2½oz/75g)
½ cup	apricot jam

Also:

1	pack Neapolitan wafers
1¾oz (50g)	vegan dark chocolate, melted

1 Preheat the oven to 350°F (180°C). For the cake layers, combine the flour, hazelnuts, sugar, baking powder, and vanilla in a bowl. In a separate bowl, mix the soy milk and canola oil, then stir into the dry ingredients until thoroughly combined. Line 2 springform pans with parchment paper and put half the mixture into each. Bake in the center of the oven for about 40 minutes, until a skewer inserted in each cake comes out clean. Remove from the oven and leave to cool completely.

2 For the filling, whip the cream with an electric mixer on its highest setting for at least 3 minutes until stiff. Put the Neapolitan wafers into a freezer bag and crush them with a rolling pin to create fine crumbs. Gradually fold the crumbs into the cream, then mix on the highest setting until well combined. Refrigerate.

3 Slice both of the cakes horizontally with a sharp knife or cheese wire to create 4 cake sections. Place one of these sections on a cake platter. Heat the apricot jam in a small pan, then spread a quarter of it on the cake, followed by a quarter of the cream, smoothing the surface to finish. Continue layering up cake, jam, and cream in this manner with the remaining sections, finishing with a mound of cream on top.

4 To decorate, chop the Neapolitan wafers into pieces and scatter them over the center of the cake, then drizzle with melted chocolate. Put the cake in the refrigerator and leave to let flavors develop overnight.

TIP:

If you'd like the cake to be even nuttier and sweeter, replace the apricot jam with vegan hazelnut spread.

FRANKFURT CROWN CAKE

For one 10½in (26cm) diameter ring mold

Time: 25 mins prep + 70 mins baking + at least 2 hrs chilling

For the cake:

4¼ cups	all-purpose flour, plus extra for dusting
1½ cups	fine cane sugar
2 tsp	baking powder
1–2	grated zest of organic lemons
1 tsp	salt
1¼ cups	canola oil
2 cups + 1 tbsp	carbonated mineral water
	vegan margarine, for greasing the mold

For the buttercream:

2 cups	vegan hazelnut drink
½ cup	instant custard powder
⅓ cup	fine cane sugar
18 tbsp	soft vegan margarine
¾ cup	soy cream, suitable for whipping

For the praline:

3 tsp	vegan margarine
¼ cup	fine cane sugar
4½oz (125g)	chopped almonds

Also:

3 tbsp	cherry jam
12	glacé cherries

1 Preheat the oven to 350°F (180°C). To make the cake, combine the flour, sugar, baking powder, lemon zest, and salt. Use a large spoon to quickly stir in the canola oil, then add the mineral water until you have a uniform mixture. Grease a ring mold with margarine and dust with flour. Transfer the cake mix into the pan and bake in the center of the oven for 70 minutes, until a skewer inserted in the cake comes out clean.

2 Meanwhile, for the buttercream, measure out about ⅔ cup of the hazelnut drink and stir in the custard powder and sugar until smooth. Bring the rest of the drink to a boil in a pan over medium heat. Remove from the stove top, stir in the custard powder mixture, then bring everything back to a boil before leaving to cool, stirring occasionally. Cream the margarine until light and fluffy, then fold it into the custard spoon by spoon. Whip the cream and fold this into the mixture.

3 For the praline, melt the margarine in a pan, add the sugar and let this dissolve, then cook until it turns brown. Stir in the almonds. Spread the mixture out over parchment paper and leave to cool, then crumble it up to create your praline. Press the cherry jam through a sieve and stir until smooth.

4 Turn the cake out from the pan and slice it to create 3 layers. Spread the bottom section with cherry jam and cover this with some of the "buttercream." Place the middle section on top and, likewise, spread with jam and buttercream. Add the final layer and cover the cake completely with the remaining buttercream, setting some aside for the final decoration.

5 Sprinkle praline all over the ring cake, pressing some of the praline carefully into the sides. Transfer the remaining buttercream into a piping bag with a star nozzle attached, and use this to pipe 12 stars on top. Decorate each star with a cherry, then chill for at least 2 hours.

TIP:
While the custard is cooling, keep stirring it to prevent a skin from forming. If a skin does develop, use a blender briefly to process it until smooth again.

GINGER COOKIE CREAM CAKE
WITH A FRUITY NOTE

For a 9½in (24cm) springform pan (12–14 pieces)

For the base:

3½oz (100g)	vegan ginger cookies
2⅓ cups	all-purpose flour
¾ cup	fine cane sugar
2 tsp	baking powder
⅓ cup	canola oil
2–3 tsp	vanilla extract
1¾ cups	carbonated mineral water

For the filling:

2⅓ cups	soy cream, suitable for whipping, well chilled
3½oz (100g)	vegan ginger cookies
2	small cans of mandarin oranges, including juice (about 1lb/450g)
2 tsp	agar-agar

For the topping:

1 cup	soy cream, suitable for whipping, well chilled
1 tsp	cream stiffener
1¾oz (50g)	vegan ginger cookies

Time: 45 mins prep + 1 hr baking

1 Preheat the oven to 325°F (160°C). For the base, pulse the ginger cookies in a food processor to create fine crumbs, or crush them in a freezer bag. Combine the cookie crumbs, flour, sugar, and baking powder in a bowl. Mix the dry ingredients with the canola oil, vanilla extract, and mineral water using a large spoon until you have a smooth consistency.

2 Line a springform pan with parchment paper, transfer the cake mix into the pan, and bake in the center of the oven for about 1 hour, until a skewer inserted in the cake comes out clean. Remove from the oven, leave to cool completely, and slice in half horizontally. Place the bottom half on a cake platter and put a cake ring around it.

3 For the filling, whip the soy cream until it is stiff. Finely crumble the ginger cookies in a freezer bag and fold the crumbs into the cream. Spread half the cream on the base and let it firm up slightly. Drain the mandarins in a sieve, catching the juice in a pan, then bring the juice to a boil with the agar-agar, stirring constantly. Lower the temperature and leave to simmer for a further 2 minutes. Allow to cool slightly, then spread the mandarins and juice over the cream layer and cover with the remaining cream. Place the upper section of your cake on top.

4 For the topping, whip the soy cream with the cream stiffener, then spread this all over the cake. There should be some cream left over. Break the ginger cookies into rough chunks and use these along with the remaining cream to add the finishing decorative touches to the cake. Chill the cake until ready to serve.

CHESTNUT LAYER CAKE
WITH HAZELNUT NOUGAT

For a 9½in (24cm) springform pan (12 pieces)

Time: 45 mins prep + 40 mins baking + at least 3 hrs chilling

For the base:

2 cups	all-purpose flour
¾ cup	fine cane sugar
2 tsp	baking powder
2 tsp	baking soda
½ tsp	salt
¼ cup	vegan cocoa powder
1¾ cups	soy milk
1½ tbsp	cider vinegar
⅔ cup	canola oil

For the filling:

2⅓ cups	soy cream, suitable for whipping, well chilled
1 tsp	(slightly heaped) agar-agar
4½oz (125g)	vegan dark chocolate, roughly chopped
5½oz (150g)	chestnut purée

Also:

6½oz (190g)	hazelnut nougat
⅔ cup	soy cream, suitable for whipping, well chilled
2¾oz (80g)	chestnut purée

1 Preheat the oven to 350°F (180°C). For the base, combine the flour, sugar, baking powder, baking soda, and salt. Sift over the cocoa powder and fold it in. Whisk together the soy milk and cider vinegar, leave to thicken for 5 minutes, then stir in the canola oil. Quickly mix the liquid and dry ingredients with a large spoon.

2 Line a springform pan with parchment paper, transfer the cake mix into the pan, and bake in the center of the oven for about 40 minutes, until a skewer inserted in the cake comes out clean. Leave to cool completely. Place the base on a cake plate and surround with a cake ring.

3 For the filling, bring 1¼ cups of the soy cream to a boil over medium heat with the agar-agar and the chocolate and simmer for a few minutes, stirring carefully, until the chocolate melts. Leave the cream to cool slightly, remembering to stir occasionally.

4 Whip the remaining soy cream for 3 minutes using an electric mixer on its highest setting. Use a hand blender to combine the chestnut purée with the warm chocolate and cream mixture. Once the chocolate cream mixture has cooled, fold in the whipped cream and spread quickly over the base of your cake. Smooth the surface with a spoon and chill thoroughly in the refrigerator for 3 hours.

5 To decorate, first melt the hazelnut nougat in a double boiler. Spread most of the nougat over the surface of your cake, then spread the remaining nougat over a board. Leave the cake and the nougat to cool. Whip the cream with the chestnut purée and transfer to a piping bag with a star nozzle attached. Cut the solidified nougat into pieces. Carefully release the cake from the ring, pipe on 12 generous swirls, and top each one with a square of the nougat.

MOUSSE AU CHOCOLAT
RASPBERRY CAKE

Uncooked but nonetheless spectacular! The cookie base is topped with a layer of enticing chocolate mousse and jewel-like raspberries.

For a 9½in (24cm) springform pan (12 pieces)

For the base:

8oz (225g)	vegan caramel cookies
8 tbsp	vegan margarine

For the filling:

14oz (400g)	vegan dark chocolate
3½ cups	soy cream, suitable for whipping, well chilled
2–3 tbsp	rum
6oz (175g) 12	raspberries, plus raspberries for decoration

Also:

½ cup	soy cream, suitable for whipping, well chilled

Time: 30 mins prep + 4 hrs chilling

1 To make the base, pulse the cookies in a food processor until you have fine crumbs. Melt the margarine and mix with the crumbs until well combined. Line a springform pan with parchment paper and spread the cookie mixture over the base, using a spoon to press it down firmly and smooth the surface. Chill for at least 2 hours.

2 For the filling, melt the dark chocolate in a double boiler and leave to cool slightly. Whip the cream with an electric mixer on its highest setting for 3 minutes, then add the chocolate. It is important for the cream to combine well with the chocolate. If required, use a spatula to scrape the chocolate from the base and sides of the bowl and stir it all through thoroughly. Flavor the mousse with the rum and beat everything again vigorously.

3 Spread half of the mousse over the cookie base. Scatter the raspberries evenly over the surface and cover with the remaining mousse, smoothing the surface. Leave to chill for a few hours.

4 Whip the cream for decorating, transfer to a piping bag with a nozzle of your choice attached, and pipe 12 large swirls of cream onto the cake. Put 1 raspberry on top of each swirl of cream. Chill until ready to serve.

TIP:

Soy cream whips more easily when it is extremely well chilled. Chill the cream the previous day and, if you prefer a firmer consistency, stir in 1 tsp of cream stiffener. If children are going to be eating this cake, simply leave out the rum.

This thoroughly chocolatey gateau with its dark sponge cake, delicate chocolate cream, and sublime raspberries will add a touch of extravagance to any dessert table.

DARK CHOCOLATE AND RASPBERRY GATEAU

For a 9½in (24cm) springform pan (12 pieces)

Time: 40 mins prep + 40 mins baking + at least 3 hrs chilling

For the base:

2 cups	all-purpose flour
¾ cup	fine cane sugar
2 tsp	baking powder
2 tsp	baking soda
½ tsp	salt
¼ cup	vegan cocoa powder
1½ tbsp	cider vinegar
1¾ cups	soy milk
⅔ cup	canola oil

For the filling:

1 lb (450g)	vegan dark chocolate
2⅓ cups	soy cream, suitable for whipping, well chilled
1 lb (450g)	raspberries (fresh or frozen), plus
2 oz (60g)	fresh raspberries, for decoration

Also:

vegan chocolate flakes

1 Preheat the oven to 350°F (180°C). For the base, combine the flour, sugar, baking powder, baking soda, and salt in a bowl. Sift over the cocoa powder and fold it in. In a separate bowl, stir the cider vinegar into the soy milk and leave to thicken for 5 minutes, then stir in the canola oil with the balloon whisk. Quickly combine the liquid and dry ingredients with a large spoon.

2 Line a springform pan with parchment paper, transfer the cake mix into the pan, and bake in the center of the oven for about 40 minutes, until a skewer inserted in the cake comes out clean. Remove from the oven and leave to cool completely.

3 Meanwhile, prepare the filling. Roughly chop the dark chocolate, melt it in a double boiler, and stir until smooth. Whip the soy cream using an electric mixer on its highest setting. Quickly beat in the chocolate until you have a uniform cream, then chill for 2–3 hours.

4 Slice the cake in half and place the lower section on a cake plate, surrounded by a cake ring. Spread a thick layer of the cream mixture on top and cover with the raspberries, followed by about half of the remaining cream mixture. Put the second cake layer on top and press down slightly. Cover the surface of the cake with the cream mixture, leaving some left over for the sides.

5 Remove the cake ring and spread the remaining cream over the sides of the gateau. Scatter with chocolate flakes. Distribute the remaining raspberries on top and refrigerate.

TIP:
Prepare a day in advance to let the flavors develop overnight in the refrigerator. Vary the fruit depending on the season; other great options include cherries (fresh or from a jar) with some kirsch drizzled over the cake.

Enjoy the vegan version of this classic recipe. Black Forest gateau is renowned for its delicate crust, flavor-packed cherries, dark sponge cake, and delicious cream.

BLACK FOREST GATEAU

For a 9½in (24cm) springform pan (12 pieces)

Time: 45 mins prep + 65 mins baking + at least 12 hrs chilling

For the filling and decoration:

3½ cups	soy cream, suitable for whipping, well chilled
10 tbsp	cream stiffener
⅔ cup	kirsch
1 tbsp	ground vanilla
25oz (720g)	jar of cherries
⅓ cup	cornstarch
2 tbsp	fine cane sugar
1–2 tsp	vanilla extract
12	Amarena cherries
	vegan dark chocolate flakes

For the crust:

½ cup	all-purpose flour
⅔ cup	ground hazelnuts
¼ cup	fine cane sugar
4 tbsp	vegan margarine
1–2 tsp	vanilla extract

For the cake mix:

2 cups	all-purpose flour
¾ cup	fine cane sugar
2 tsp	baking powder
½ tsp	salt
2 tsp	baking soda
¼ cup	vegan cocoa powder
1½ tbsp	cider vinegar
1¾ cups	soy milk
⅔ cup	canola oil

1 For the filling, whip the soy cream with an electric mixer on its highest setting for 2 minutes. Beat in the cream stiffener, ½ cup of the kirsch, and the vanilla. Set in the refrigerator to chill. Preheat the oven to 350°F (180°C). For the crust, combine the flour, hazelnuts, and sugar. Use your fingers to work in the margarine, then mix in the vanilla extract. Transfer to a springform pan lined with parchment paper. Smooth out the pastry and prick all over with a fork. Bake in the oven for 20–25 minutes. Leave to cool completely.

2 For the cake mixture, combine the flour, sugar, baking powder, salt, and baking soda. Sift in the cocoa powder. Stir the cider vinegar into the soy milk, leave to thicken for 5 minutes, then stir in the canola oil. Quickly combine the liquid and dry ingredients with a large spoon. Transfer to a springform pan lined with parchment paper and bake in the center of the oven for 40 minutes. Leave to cool completely, then slice in half horizontally. Put a cake ring securely around the crust base.

3 For the filling, drain the cherries but retain the juice. Mix half the juice with the cornstarch, sugar, and vanilla extract. Bring the other half to a boil, remove the pan from the stove top, stir in the cornstarch and juice mixture, then return to a boil while stirring. Remove from the heat again. Stir in the cherries. Once the mixture has cooled slightly, spread it over the crust.

4 Place one of the cake layers on top of the cherries and press down slightly. Drizzle the cake with 2 tablespoons kirsch, then spread one third of the cream on top. Cover with the second cake layer, drizzle with 2 tablespoons kirsch, spread with cream, and chill briefly. Release from the cake ring and cover the sides with cream. Transfer the remaining cream to a piping bag with a star nozzle attached and pipe 12 swirls on top. Top each swirl with an Amarena cherry. Scatter chocolate flakes over top and chill overnight.

GLUTEN-FREE

CREPE LAYER CAKE

A quick, gluten-free alternative to a cake or gateau. Using fresh seasonal fruit with a soft coconut cream creates a colorful and tasty treat.

Serves 12–14

Time: 1 hr

For the batter:

2 cups	buckwheat flour
1 tsp	baking powder
½	seeds scraped from vanilla bean
2 tbsp	fine cane sugar
1	pinch of sea salt
2⅓ cups	cold carbonated mineral water

Also:

2⅓ cups	coconut cream, suitable for whipping, well chilled
14oz (400g)	strawberries
¼ cup	canola oil, for cooking
½ cup	strawberry jam
	coconut flakes, to decorate

1 In a large bowl, combine the buckwheat flour and baking powder. Stir in the vanilla seeds, sugar, and sea salt. Add the mineral water and mix to create a batter. Leave to stand for 20 minutes.

2 Meanwhile, whip the coconut cream and then chill it in the refrigerator. Trim and quarter the strawberries.

3 Heat some canola oil in a pan. Add a ladle of crepe batter to the pan, spreading it out slightly. As soon as the edges have cooked firm and turned golden, flip the crepe and cook until golden on the other side. Continue in this manner until all the batter has been used.

4 Leave the crepes to cool completely. Layer them up, spreading each one with jam, whipped cream, and then toping it with strawberries. Finish with a scatter of coconut flakes over the top layer.

TIP:

Coconut cream tastes particularly delicious if you fold in a few tablespoons of toasted coconut flakes. To do this, toast the coconut flakes in a dry pan over medium heat until golden. Take care, as coconut flakes burn very quickly.

CHOCOLATE CAKE WITH BANANA

For a 9½in (24cm) springform pan (12–14 pieces)

Time: 40 mins prep + 12 hrs draining + 40 mins baking

For the banana cream:

2¼lb (1kg)	soy yogurt
1¼ cups	soy cream, suitable for whipping, well chilled
2 tbsp	fine cane sugar
1–2 tsp	vanilla extract
3 tbsp	cream stiffener
2	medium-sized ripe bananas

For decorating:

½ cup	soy cream, suitable for whipping, well chilled
2¾oz (80g)	vegan dark chocolate, chopped
	banana chips, roughly chopped

For the base:

2 cups	all-purpose flour
¾ cup	fine cane sugar
2 tsp	baking powder
2 tsp	baking soda
½ tsp	salt
¼ cup	vegan cocoa powder
1½ tbsp	cider vinegar
1¾ cups	soy milk
⅔ cup	canola oil

For the filling:

4	medium bananas
1¾ cups	banana juice drink
2 tsp	vegan clear cake glaze

1 For the banana cream, put the soy yogurt into a sieve lined with a thick paper towel and leave to drain overnight into a bowl. For decorating, whip the cream until stiff. Melt the chocolate in a double boiler and fold it into the cream. Refrigerate overnight.

2 To make the base, first preheat the oven to 350°F (180°C). Combine the flour, sugar, baking powder, baking soda, and salt. Sift over the cocoa powder and fold it in. Stir the cider vinegar into the soy milk, leave to thicken for 5 minutes, then stir in the canola oil. Quickly stir together the liquid and dry ingredients with a spoon. Transfer to a springform pan lined with parchment paper and bake for about 40 minutes. Leave to cool, transfer to a cake plate, and surround with a cake ring.

3 For the filling, peel the bananas, slice thickly, and spread them over the base. In a small pan, prepare the banana juice with the cake glaze, following the instructions on the glaze package. As soon as it has thickened, spread the mixture over the bananas and transfer the cake to the fridge to chill.

4 For the banana cream, squeeze out the drained soy yogurt and put it into a bowl. Whip the soy cream using an electric mixer on its highest setting, then stir in the sugar, vanilla extract, and cream stiffener. Peel the bananas, mash with a fork to a fine purée, and fold this into the cream. Add the yogurt and stir everything to a smooth, firm consistency. Spread this over the glazed bananas and smooth the surface. Chill the whole cake again.

5 Transfer the chocolate cream into a piping bag with a star nozzle attached. Pipe swirls around the edge of the cake and sprinkle them with banana chips. Carefully release the cake ring with the help of a sharp knife and chill the cake until ready to serve.

CHOCOLATE TART

RAW & GLUTEN-FREE

For a 11in (28cm) tart pan (12 pieces)

Time: 20 mins prep + 1 day soaking + 2 hrs chilling

For the base:

3½oz (100g)	whole blanched almonds
10oz (300g)	dates, pitted
5½oz (150g)	walnuts
2 tbsp	vegan cocoa powder

For the chocolate cream:

2	avocados (Hass variety)
2	very ripe bananas
7	dates, pitted
5 tbsp	vegan cocoa powder
1 tsp	orange juice, freshly squeezed

Also:

1¼oz (40g)	fine coconut flakes, for sprinkling

1 For the base, soak the almonds in plenty of water the day before. Leave the almonds to drain well, then chop roughly in a food processor. Add all the ingredients for the base and process everything until you have a uniform mixture. Sprinkle the tart pan with coconut flakes. Transfer the almond mixture into the tart pan, spreading it out to a ½–¾in (1–2cm) thickness and creating a slight rim around the edge. Leave it to chill in the refrigerator.

2 For the chocolate cream, halve the avocados, remove the pits, and use a tablespoon to scoop out the flesh. Add to a food processor. Peel the bananas and roughly break into pieces. Add the bananas, dates, cocoa powder, and orange juice to the avocados and process everything to a smooth and creamy consistency. Spread this over the base and smooth the surface. Before serving, chill the tart for about 2 hours in the refrigerator or, if you're short on time, about 1 hour in the freezer.

GLUTEN-FREE

COCONUT TART
WITH CHOCOLATE

This delicious gluten-free tart is simple to prepare and tastes absolutely heavenly, so it will be popular with everyone, not just fans of coconut and chocolate.

For a 9½in (24cm) tart pan (12 pieces)

Time: 25 mins prep + 15 mins baking + chilling time

For the base:
6 tbsp	coconut oil
9½oz (280g)	coconut flakes
¾ cup	agave syrup

For the filling:
10oz (300g)	vegan dark chocolate
1 cup	coconut milk

Also:
vegan margarine, for greasing the pan

coconut flakes

soy cream, suitable for whipping, well chilled (optional)

1 Preheat the oven to 350°F (180°C). For the base, melt the coconut oil in a small pan over low heat, then set aside. Use a spoon to stir the coconut flakes and agave syrup together in a bowl. Knead in the slightly cooled coconut oil with your fingers.

2 Grease a tart pan with margarine. Transfer your mixture to a pan, creating a thick rim about 1½in (3cm) high. Smooth the base with a spoon, pressing everything down firmly. Bake in the center of the oven for about 15 minutes, until the sides and base are pale brown—but not too dark. Remove from the oven and leave to cool slightly until the base is firm.

3 For the filling, roughly chop the dark chocolate. Bring the coconut milk to a boil in a pan over medium heat and stir in the chocolate, until you have a smooth consistency and there are no more lumps. Pour the chocolate cream into the base and chill the tart in the fridge for several hours, until set.

4 Toast the coconut flakes in a dry pan, then scatter over the tart. Whip the soy cream, if using, with an electric mixer on its highest setting. Use the cream to decorate the tart. Serve well chilled.

TIP:
This tart is made without any flour and also contains very little sugar. Dark chocolate with a cocoa content of at least 70 percent is ideal for this recipe.

This splendid tart is incredibly versatile! The base can be combined with any fruit for a delicious treat; whether you use apples, pears, or a thick layer of berries—this is a tart for all seasons.

WHOLE-GRAIN TART
WITH SEASONAL FRUIT

For a 9½in (24cm) tart pan (12 pieces)

Time: 30 mins prep + 30 mins chilling + 45 mins baking

For the base:

2 cups	whole-grain spelt flour, plus extra for dusting
⅓ cup	fine cane sugar
1 tsp	vanilla powder
1 tsp	baking powder
1	pinch of salt
1	grated zest of small organic lemon
1 tbsp	ground flax seed
6 tbsp	vegan margarine, plus extra for greasing the pan

For the crumble:

1 cup	whole-grain spelt flour
½ cup	fine cane sugar
1 tsp	vanilla powder
8 tbsp	vegan margarine

For the filling:

½ cup	ground almonds
1lb 2oz (500g)	seasonal fruit, washed and chopped

Also:

powdered sugar, to dust

1 For the base, combine the flour, cane sugar, vanilla powder, baking powder, salt, and lemon zest in a bowl. Stir the flax seed together with 3 tablespoons of water and leave to swell for 5 minutes. Add little blobs of margarine to the flour mixture and use your fingers to rub it in, then add the flax seed to create a smooth pastry mixture. Grease a tart pan and dust with flour. Transfer your pastry into the pan, pressing it out to cover the bottom and create a rim around the edge, and prick all over with a fork. Chill the pastry for at least 30 minutes.

2 Preheat the oven to 350°F (180°C). Meanwhile, for the crumble, combine the flour, cane sugar, and vanilla powder in a bowl and carefully rub in the margarine. Use your fingers to create rough crumble pieces.

3 For the filling, spread the almonds over the base and cover with the fruit. Top with the crumble and bake the tart in the center of the oven for 35–45 minutes. Remove, leave to cool, and dust with powdered sugar.

TIP:

This tart tastes delicious with a custard layer. Prepare a custard made from 1½ cups soy milk, 3 tbsp cane sugar, 2–3 tsp vanilla extract, and ⅓ cup cornstarch. Spread the custard over the base of the tart instead of the almonds, then add the fruit layer on top. Scatter over the crumble and bake as described.

FILLING FOOD AND SNACKS

From pizza, to quiche, to rolls: delicious, hearty, meat-free food; tasty party snacks and nibbles; and nutritious breads for baking enthusiasts.

HAWAIIAN PIZZA

For a 12 × 15½in (30 × 40cm) baking sheet

Time: 20 mins prep + 55 mins proofing + 25 mins baking

For the dough:

2¼ tsp	dried yeast
2¼ cups	spelt flour with a high gluten content, plus extra for dusting
1 tsp	salt
1	pinch of fine cane sugar
2 tbsp	olive oil

For the sauce:

14oz (400g)	tomato purée
3½oz (100g)	tomato paste
1 tbsp	olive oil
1 tsp	sea salt
½ tsp	ground white pepper
1	pinch of fine cane sugar
1	squeeze lemon juice
1 tsp	dried oregano

For the topping:

4½oz (125g)	smoked tofu or vegan ham
8	pineapple slices
	oregano leaves, for scattering

For the "cheese":

5 tbsp	cashew nut butter
2 tsp	yeast flakes
½ tsp	salt
¼ tsp	ground white pepper
1	squeeze lemon juice

1 To make the dough, put ¾ cup lukewarm water into a bowl and sprinkle the yeast over the top. Cover and leave at room temperature for about 10 minutes, then use a balloon whisk to mix to a smooth consistency.

2 In a separate large bowl, combine the spelt flour, salt, and sugar. Add the olive oil and the yeast and water mixture, and knead everything until you have a smooth dough. Cover and leave to proof for about 45 minutes, until doubled in size.

3 Meanwhile, for the sauce, stir together the tomato purée, tomato paste, and olive oil. Season to taste with the sea salt, pepper, sugar, lemon juice, and oregano.

4 For the topping, roughly dice the tofu or ham. For the "cheese," stir 3 tablespoons of water into the cashew nut butter. Add the yeast flakes, salt, pepper, and lemon juice to taste.

5 Preheat the oven to 400°F (200°C) and line a baking sheet with parchment paper. Knead the dough vigorously once more and roll it out on a work surface dusted with flour until it is the size of the baking sheet. Spread the tomato sauce, topping, and then the "cheese" over the dough. Bake the pizza in the center of the oven for 20–25 minutes until golden brown. Remove, slice into 12 portions, and scatter with oregano leaves before serving.

TIP:

This pizza also tastes delicious with pickled tofu, strips of pepper and onion, cherry tomatoes, mushrooms, or pumpkin.

TARTE FLAMBÉE

With a crisp, thin base topped with delicious pointed cabbage, this vegan tarte flambée is just as good as the original!

For a 12 × 15½in (30 × 40cm) baking sheet

Time: 15 mins prep + 2 hrs proofing + 25 mins baking

For the dough:

1¾ cups	all-purpose flour
½ tsp	salt
1	pinch of fine cane sugar
½ cup	mild-tasting soy milk
2 tbsp	olive oil

For the topping:

10oz (300g)	pointed cabbage
3	onions
1	carrot
7oz (200g)	smoked tofu or smoked tempeh
2 tbsp	canola oil
1 tsp	salt
½ tsp	freshly ground white pepper
1	pinch of grated nutmeg
½ tsp	caraway seeds

Also:

7oz (200g)	vegan crème fraîche
¾oz (20g)	pine nuts

1 To make the dough, combine the flour, salt, and sugar in a bowl. Add the soy milk and olive oil and knead everything vigorously until you have a uniform, soft dough. Cover and leave the dough to proof in a warm place for at least 2 hours.

2 Meanwhile, for the topping, halve the pointed cabbage, cut out the stalk in a V-shaped wedge, and slice the cabbage into roughly ½in (1cm) wide strips. Peel the onions and carrot, cut in half, and slice into thin strips. Dice the smoked tofu.

3 Heat the canola oil in a large nonstick pan over high heat and sear the tofu until it is nice and crisp. Reduce the heat and add the pointed cabbage, carrot, and onions. Cook over medium heat, stirring frequently, being sure not to let the vegetables color too much. Season with the salt, pepper, nutmeg, and caraway seeds.

4 Preheat the oven to 400°F (200°C). Knead the dough vigorously again, divide into two portions, and roll these out as thinly as possible. Lay the pieces on a baking sheet lined with parchment paper and cover with a thin layer of crème fraîche. Spread the topping out evenly, then drizzle over the remaining crème fraîche. Bake the tarte flambée in the center of the oven for 20–25 minutes, until slightly crisp and golden brown. Scatter the pine nuts over the tart about 10 minutes before the end of the baking time. Remove from the oven and enjoy while still warm.

123

The combination of savoy cabbage, lentils, and tomatoes on a yeast dough is quite simply brilliant. You've just got to give it a try!

SAVOY CABBAGE TART

For a 12 × 15½in (30 × 40cm) baking sheet

Time: 45 mins prep + 55 mins proofing + 35 mins baking

For the dough:

1 tsp	dried yeast
2¼ cups	spelt flour with a high gluten content
1 tsp	salt
1	pinch of fine cane sugar
2 tbsp	olive oil

For the topping:

3oz (85g)	dried brown lentils
14oz (400g)	savoy cabbage
2	onions
2	garlic cloves
3½oz (100g)	tomato paste
3½ tbsp	red wine or vegetable stock
17oz (500g)	can chopped tomatoes
1	pinch of herbal salt and freshly ground black pepper
½ tsp	sweet paprika
1	pinch of grated nutmeg
	juice of ½ lemon

Also:

3½ tbsp	olive oil, for frying

1 To make the dough, sprinkle the yeast into a bowl containing ¾ cup lukewarm water. Cover and leave to proof in a warm place for about 10 minutes, then whisk until smooth with a balloon whisk. Combine the flour, salt, and sugar in a large bowl. Add the olive oil and the water and yeast mixture and work until you have a smooth dough. Cover and leave to proof in a warm place for 30–45 minutes, until doubled in size.

2 Meanwhile, for the topping, cook the lentils according to the package instructions, strain off the water, and leave to drain. Remove the stalk from the savoy cabbage and slice into diamonds. Peel and finely dice the onions and garlic. Heat the olive oil in a large pan, add the savoy cabbage, and sauté over high heat. Add the onions, garlic, and tomato paste and cook briefly. Quickly deglaze with red wine and add the tomatoes. Season to taste with the herbal salt, pepper, paprika, nutmeg, and lemon juice. Finally, fold in the lentils.

3 Preheat the oven to 400°F (200°C) and line a baking sheet with parchment paper. Knead the dough again vigorously and roll it out on the baking sheet. Spread the savoy cabbage and lentil mixture on top and bake in the center of the oven for 30–35 minutes. Remove and enjoy while still warm.

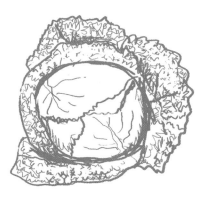

ONION TART

This tart is easy to make, filling, and tastes fabulous!

For a 12 × 15½in (30 × 40cm) baking sheet

For the dough:

1 tsp	dried yeast
2¼ cups	spelt flour with a high gluten content, plus extra for dusting
2 tbsp	olive oil
1 tsp	salt
1	pinch of fine cane sugar

For the topping:

8	onions
1	garlic clove
1	long leek
1–2	red bell peppers
4 tbsp	vegan margarine
¾ cup	vegetable stock
1¼ cups	oat cream, well chilled
5 tsp	almond butter
½ cup	yeast flakes
1 tbsp	caraway seeds
1 tsp	salt and freshly ground black pepper

Time: 20 mins prep + 1 hr proofing + 45 mins baking

1 To make the dough, put ¾ cup lukewarm water into a large bowl, sprinkle in the yeast, and use a balloon whisk to dissolve it in the water. Add the flour, olive oil, salt, and sugar and knead everything until you have a uniform dough. If the dough is too sticky, add a bit more flour. Wrap the dough in plastic wrap and put it in the refrigerator for at least 1 hour.

2 For the topping, peel the onions and garlic. Slice the leek and onions into very fine rings, mince the garlic, and dice the bell peppers. In a high-sided pan, melt the margarine over medium heat and sauté the leek, onions, and garlic. Add the diced bell pepper, dust with flour, and continue to sauté briefly. Gradually add the vegetable stock, oat cream, and almond butter and thicken slightly, stirring constantly. Season to taste with the yeast flakes, caraway seeds, and salt and pepper.

3 Preheat the oven to 400°F (200°C). Line a baking sheet with parchment paper and roll out the dough on it. Prick the dough with a fork, then top with the leek and onion mixture. Bake the onion tart in the center of the oven for 40–45 minutes until golden; it is ready if the crust sounds hollow when tapped. Remove and enjoy while still warm.

TIP:

If you really feel this dish could do with some "bacon," replace the bell peppers with 7oz (200g) chopped mushrooms, drizzle with 2 tbsp olive oil and soy sauce, and season with pepper. Spread on the tart before baking.

QUICHE LORRAINE

For a 9½in (24cm) springform pan (12–14 pieces)

Time: 30 mins prep + 1 hr chilling + 35 mins baking

For the pastry:

2 cups	all-purpose flour, plus extra for dusting
1 tsp	salt
10 tbsp	vegan margarine

For the filling:

5½oz (150g)	smoked tofu
1	garlic clove
10	scallions
1 cup	soy cream
5½oz (150g)	vegan cheese, grated
1 tsp	salt
½ tsp	freshly ground black pepper
½ tsp	ground turmeric
1	pinch of grated nutmeg

Also:

3 tbsp	canola oil, for frying

1 For the pastry, combine the flour with the salt. Add the margarine in little blobs and work it in with your fingers. Gradually add ½ cup water and combine everything until you have a smooth crust. Wrap in plastic wrap and put in the refrigerator for about 1 hour.

2 Roll out the pastry on a surface dusted with flour and transfer it into a springform pan lined with parchment paper or a well-greased quiche pan dusted with flour. Shape the pastry to create a 2in (5cm) high edge, press it down firmly, and prick with a fork. Put the pan in the refrigerator to chill while you prepare the filling.

3 Cut the smoked tofu into little cubes and finely chop the garlic. Slice the scallions into thin rings. Heat the oil over high heat in a nonstick pan and briefly sear the tofu cubes, then reduce to medium heat and sauté the cubes until brown on all sides. Add the scallions and finally the garlic and continue to cook briefly. Tip the contents of the pan onto a large plate lined with paper towel and let the excess fat drain away.

4 Preheat the oven to 350°F (180°C). In a large bowl, combine the soy cream with the cheese and season with the salt, pepper, turmeric, and nutmeg. Fold in the tofu mixture and spread everything over the quiche base, smoothing the surface. Bake the quiche in the center of the oven for 30–35 minutes. Remove and enjoy while still warm.

TIP:

Instead of store-bought vegan cheese, you can also use the cashew nut "cheese" from the Hawaiian pizza (see p.120).

Macadamia nuts introduce a bit of bite and, along with the slightly astringent arugula, combine beautifully with the delicate spinach and tomato filling.

SPINACH QUICHE

For a 11in (28cm) springform pan (12–14 pieces)

Time: 20 mins prep + 1 hr chilling + 1 hr baking

For the pastry:

2¼ cups	spelt flour with a high gluten content
10 tbsp	vegan margarine, plus extra for greasing the pan
1 tsp	salt
1	pinch of cane sugar

For the filling:

1 tbsp	vegan margarine
1lb (450g)	spinach leaves (frozen)
1	onion
1	garlic clove
7oz (200g)	cherry tomatoes
1¼ cups	spelt cream (available online)
3½oz (100g)	vegan cheese, grated
1 tsp	salt
½ tsp	freshly ground black pepper
1	pinch of freshly grated nutmeg
scant 1oz (25g)	macadamia nuts

Also:

3½oz (100g)	arugula
2 tbsp	olive oil, to drizzle

1 To make the pastry, combine the flour, margarine, salt, sugar, and ½ cup of water in a bowl until it forms a dough. Wrap the pastry in plastic wrap and chill in the refrigerator for 1 hour. Grease a springform pan, roll out the pastry, and place it in the pan. Shape the pastry so that the sides come up to create a border.

2 Preheat the oven to 400°F (200°C). For the filling, melt the margarine in a large high-sided pan. Add the spinach and sauté over low heat. Peel the onion and garlic, dice finely, and add to the spinach. Halve the cherry tomatoes and add these, too. Pour in the cream and add the vegan cheese.

3 Season the filling to taste with salt, pepper, and the nutmeg and pour it into the pastry case. Bake the quiche in the center of the oven for 50–60 minutes until golden. Chop the macadamias and scatter over the quiche about 10 minutes before the end of the cooking time. Remove the quiche and release from the pan to serve, scatter with the arugula, and drizzle with olive oil.

"Pide," a type of Turkish flatbread, is a delicious alternative to pizza and is just as versatile as its Italian relative when it comes to toppings. The main difference is the shape.

PIDES

Makes 2 pides

Time: 25 mins prep + 45 mins proofing + 15 mins baking

For the dough:

1¾ cups	all-purpose flour
¾ tsp	dried yeast
1	pinch of fine cane sugar
1 tsp	salt

For the topping:

7oz (200g)	spinach leaves (frozen)
7oz (200g)	broccoli florets (frozen)
3½oz (100g)	peas (frozen)
1	pinch of salt
1	small onion
1	small red pepper
½ cup	oat cream
	freshly ground black pepper, to taste
2 tbsp	pine nuts

Also:

3½ tbsp	soy milk
1¾oz (50g)	sesame seeds

1 To make the dough, combine the flour with the yeast, sugar, and salt in a bowl. Add ⅔ cup water and knead into a smooth dough. Cover and leave to proof in a warm place for 30–45 minutes, until doubled in size.

2 Preheat the oven to 400°F (200°C) and line a baking sheet with parchment paper. Halve the dough and roll out each piece on the baking sheet until they are about a finger-width thick. The dough should be oval, with the ends tapering to a point.

3 For the topping, briefly blanch the spinach, broccoli, and peas in slightly salted boiling water, then drain. Peel the onion and slice into thin rings, then seed the pepper and chop it into cubes. Spread both pides with the oat cream and top with the vegetables, seasoning to taste. Scatter with the pine nuts, then gently fold up the edges of the dough. Brush the edges of the pides with some soy milk, scatter with the sesame seeds, and bake in the center of the oven for 15 minutes. Remove and enjoy while still warm.

Savory muffins are a great snack, and also a fabulous dish to take to a celebration or cookout. The delicious spelt flour with smoked tofu offers something new in terms of flavor.

SAVORY MUFFINS

Makes 12 muffins

Time: 25 mins prep + 25 mins baking

3½oz (100g)	smoked tofu
1	red onion
3 tbsp	canola oil, for frying
1¼ cups	spelt flour
1 tsp	baking powder
1 tsp	salt
½ tsp	freshly ground black pepper
1 tsp	sweet paprika
10 tbsp	vegan margarine
3½ tbsp	unsweetened soy milk

1 Finely dice the tofu and the red onion. Heat the canola oil over medium heat in a nonstick pan. Sauté the tofu and onion.

2 Preheat the oven to 350°F (180°C). Put paper liners into the wells of a muffin pan. In a large bowl, combine the flour with the baking powder and the spices. Add the margarine in little blobs and rub it in with your fingers. Gradually incorporate the soy milk, followed by the onion and tofu mixture.

3 Transfer the mixture into the muffin liners and bake in the center of the oven for 20–25 minutes, until a skewer inserted in a muffin comes out clean. Remove from the oven. You can eat the muffins warm or cold.

TIP:

Instead of smoked tofu, you could also dice 3½oz (100g) sweet potatoes, marinate them in soy sauce, and sauté with the onions. For a really wonderful smoky aroma, try using smoked paprika.

Ready in a flash, these herby straws will be gobbled up instantly by party guests!

PARTY STRAWS

Makes 30 straws

Time: 20 mins prep + 20 mins baking

For the party straws:

5	store-bought puff pastry sheets (6 × 6in/15 × 15cm each), see pp.14–15; chilled
1¼oz (40g)	vegan cheese, grated
1 heaped tsp	caraway seeds
1 heaped tsp	coarse sea salt
1 heaped tsp	dried rosemary

Also:

3½ tbsp	soy milk, for brushing

1 Cut each puff pastry sheet into 6 equal-sized strips. Brush each of the 30 strips with soy milk. Scatter equal quantities of cheese and caraway seeds over half of the pastry strips and scatter the other half with sea salt and rosemary.

2 Preheat the oven to 350°C (180°C). Twist the pastry strips and place them on a baking sheet lined with parchment paper. Bake the straws in the center of the oven for 15–20 minutes until golden. Remove and eat when they are lukewarm or cold.

TIP:

It's important to work quickly with the puff pastry, while it is still cold. You can also make a sweet version of these party straws by sprinkling them with cinnamon sugar.

CIABATTA ROLLS

Makes 8–10 rolls

Time: 10 mins prep + 65 mins proofing + 20 mins baking

2¼ tsp	active dry yeast
2 cups	all-purpose flour, plus extra for dusting
2 tbsp	olive oil
1 tsp	salt
½ tsp	fine cane sugar
3½ tbsp	soy milk, for brushing (optional)

1 Pour ⅔ cup lukewarm water into a large bowl. Sprinkle the yeast over the water, cover, and leave in a warm place to rest for about 10 minutes. Combine with a balloon whisk, then add the flour, olive oil, salt, and sugar and knead until it forms a supple dough. Cover and leave to proof in a warm place for 30–45 minutes, until doubled in size.

2 Preheat the oven to 400°F (200°C). On a floured work surface, shape the dough into a long log and roll this out until it is about a finger-width thick. To make the ciabatta rolls, cut this sheet into 8–10 equal-sized rectangles, cover, and leave to proof for a further 20 minutes.

3 Either dust the ciabatta rolls with flour or, if you prefer a smooth surface, brush with soy milk. Bake the rolls in the center of the oven for 15–20 minutes. Remove and leave to cool slightly.

When you need a recipe that is both quick to make and healthy, these Kamut® rolls are just perfect. Kamut® is a nutrient-rich, ancient variety of wheat that is once again being cultivated today.

SPEEDY WHOLE-GRAIN ROLLS

Makes 20 rolls

Time: 10 mins prep + 10 mins proofing + 25 mins baking

For the dough:

2¼ tsp	active dry yeast
5¼ cups	Kamut®, freshly milled, or whole-wheat flour
1 tsp	sea salt
½ tsp	ground allspice
1 tsp	ground turmeric

Also:

3½ tbsp	soy milk, for brushing
	pumpkin seeds, poppy seeds, or sesame seeds, for sprinkling (optional)

1 Sprinkle the yeast into a bowl containing 2 cups lukewarm water, cover, and leave in a warm place for 10 minutes. Combine the flour, sea salt, allspice, and turmeric in a separate bowl. Whisk the yeast and water and add to the flour mixture. Knead everything until it forms a smooth dough.

2 Preheat the oven to 400°F (200°C) and line a baking sheet with parchment paper. Form around 20 equal-sized rolls from the dough, place them on the baking sheet, brush with soy milk, and sprinkle with the seeds of your choice, if using. Bake the rolls in the center of the oven for about 25 minutes. Remove and leave to cool slightly.

TIP:
If you spray the rolls with water halfway through the baking time, this makes the crust nice and crunchy. These rolls are perfect for freezing.

PUMPKIN AND BUCKWHEAT ROLLS

Makes 12 rolls

3¾ cups	buckwheat flour
1 tsp	cream of tartar
2 tbsp	guar gum
1 tsp	sea salt
½ tsp	ground allspice
1	pinch of ground aniseed
3½ tbsp	flax seed oil
2 cups	carbonated mineral water
3½oz (100g)	pumpkin seeds

Time: 10 mins prep + 30 mins baking

1 In a large bowl, combine the flour with the cream of tartar, guar gum, sea salt, allspice, and aniseed. Add the flax seed oil and mineral water and work everything together until it forms a smooth dough. Knead in the pumpkin seeds.

2 Preheat the oven to 400°F (200°C) and line a baking sheet with parchment paper. Divide the dough into 12 equal-sized portions and shape these into oval rolls. Place the rolls on the baking sheet and make several diagonal incisions in the surface of each one. Bake the rolls in the center of the oven for about 30 minutes. Remove and leave to cool slightly. These rolls are also perfect for freezing.

TIP:

Take care when shopping to buy baking powder that is explicitly labeled as gluten-free. Some baking powders continue to include tiny amounts of wheat flour. Gluten-free products are often labeled with a crossed-out ear of wheat.

Muesli to go! This recipe takes your favorite muesli and transforms it into an easy-to-transport bread roll, which is ideal for when you're on the move.

MUESLI ROLLS

Makes 6 rolls

2¾ cups	whole-grain spelt flour
5½oz (150g)	muesli of your choice
¾ tsp	salt
1 cup + 2 tbsp	almond milk, plus extra for brushing
1½ tbsp	agave syrup
2¼ tsp	active dry yeast
2 tbsp	vegan margarine

Time: 20 mins prep + 85 mins proofing + 30 mins baking

1 Combine the flour, muesli, and salt in a large bowl. Warm the almond milk over low heat and pour it into a separate bowl. Stir in the agave syrup, sprinkle in the yeast, and stir everything gently. Cover and leave in a warm place for about 10 minutes.

2 Melt the margarine in a pan and add to the flour and muesli mixture. Stir the almond milk and yeast mixture once again, then add this to the dough mixture. Knead everything thoroughly to form a smooth, pliable dough—if necessary, add a bit more almond milk. Cover and leave the dough to proof in a warm place for 45 minutes, until doubled in size.

3 Shape 6 rolls from the dough, make an X in the top of each one, and leave to proof for a further 30 minutes.

4 Preheat the oven to 400°F (200°C). Brush the rolls with some almond milk and bake in the center of the oven for 20–30 minutes. Remove from the oven and leave to cool slightly.

SESAME BAGELS

Makes 10 bagels

Time: 25 mins prep + 85 mins proofing + 15 mins baking

2¾ cups	bread flour, plus extra for dusting
1 tsp	salt
1 tbsp	vegan margarine
2¼ tsp	active dry yeast
1 tsp	fine cane sugar
3½ tbsp	soy milk, for brushing
3 tbsp	pale sesame seeds

1 Add the flour and salt to a large bowl and create a well in the center. Warm the margarine with 1 cup + 2 tbsp water in a small pan over low heat until it has melted. Leave the mixture to cool a little until it's lukewarm. Sprinkle in the yeast and add the sugar. Cover the mixture and leave to stand for about 10 minutes, then combine with a balloon whisk and pour into the well in the center of the flour. Knead everything until it forms a smooth dough. Shape the dough into a ball, cover, and leave to proof in a warm place for about 45 minutes, until doubled in size.

2 Dust your work surface with flour. Divide the dough as evenly as possible into 10 pieces and shape these into balls. Use the handle of a wooden spoon to make a hole in the center of each ball to create a ring, then use your fingers to widen the hole in each dough ring to about ¾–1½in (2–3cm).

3 Line a baking sheet with parchment paper and place the bagels on it. Leave to proof for another 30 minutes. Brush the tops of the bagels with soy milk and scatter evenly with sesame seeds. Set the oven to 450°F (230°C); do not preheat. Put the bagels into the center of the cold oven and bake for about 15 minutes. Remove and leave to cool on a wire rack.

TIP:

If you make bagels regularly, you can buy a special tool that lets you quickly mold the bagels so they are all the same size and shape.

This potato bread is soft and moist and tastes equally great with sweet or savory toppings. It also stays fresh for several days.

SOFT POTATO BREAD

Makes 1 medium-sized loaf

Time: 40 mins prep + 2¼ hrs proofing + 30 mins baking

For the yeast starter mix:

⅔ cup	soy milk
2 heaped tsp	everything spice
⅓ cup	spelt flour
1 tsp	dried yeast
1 tbsp	agave syrup

For the main dough:

½ cup	soy milk
3 tbsp	soy yogurt
1	squeeze lemon juice
2¾ cups	spelt flour, plus extra for dusting
1½ tsp	salt
10oz (300g)	potatoes, peeled and cooked

1 To make the starter mix, warm the soy milk in a pan with the everything spice and then set aside. Combine the flour and dried yeast in a bowl. Stir the agave syrup into the spiced soy milk, then mix everything into the dry ingredients until well combined. Cover and leave to proof in a warm place for about 15 minutes, then stir until smooth again.

2 For the main dough, whisk together the soy milk, soy yogurt, and lemon juice, then warm over low heat. Remove from the heat. Combine the flour and salt in a bowl. Mash the potatoes and add them to the flour. Stir in the soy milk, yogurt, and lemon juice mixture. Then add the starter mix and knead everything until you have a smooth dough, possibly adding a bit of soy milk or flour, if required. Cover and leave to proof in a warm place for about 1 hour, until doubled in size.

3 Knead the dough vigorously and shape it into an oval loaf. Place this on a baking sheet lined with parchment paper, dust with flour, and leave to proof again for about 1 hour. Preheat the oven to 400°F (200°C). Make 4 incisions in the top of the loaf and bake in the center of the oven for 30 minutes. If the bread begins to darken too quickly, cover it with foil. Remove and leave to cool.

TIP:

If the bread sounds hollow when you tap on the base, it is ready. You can make your own delicious bread spice by finely grinding fennel, coriander, caraway, cardamom, aniseed, and blue fenugreek using a pestle and mortar.

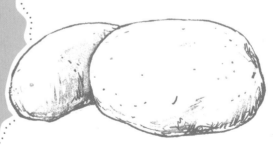

Packed with nutrients, full of flavor, and super quick to bake, this tasty bread is ideal for those with a gluten intolerance.

PUMPKIN AND AMARANTH BREAD

For a 11in (28cm) long loaf pan

2 cups	buckwheat flour, plus extra for dusting
⅓ cup	puffed amaranth
2 tbsp	ground sesame seeds
1 tsp	baking powder
½ tsp	sea salt
1 tsp	ground turmeric
2 tsp	guar gum
2 tbsp	olive oil
2 cups	carbonated mineral water
3½oz (100g)	pumpkin seeds
	vegan margarine, for greasing the pan

Time: 25 minutes prep + 35 minutes baking

1 Combine the flour with the amaranth, sesame seeds, baking powder, sea salt, turmeric, and guar gum in a bowl. Add the olive oil and mineral water and knead everything quickly to form a smooth dough. Work in the pumpkin seeds.

2 Preheat the oven to 400°F (200°C). Transfer the dough to a greased loaf pan dusted with flour and bake in the center of the oven for 30–35 minutes, until a skewer inserted in the bread comes out clean. Remove and leave to cool completely in the pan before turning out the loaf.

TIP:

If you can't find ground sesame seeds, you can also use the whole seeds. Just reduce the quantity of liquid slightly or adjust the amount of flour accordingly.

This delicious bread is a huge hit thanks to the nutritious spelt, the vitamin-rich carrots, and the healthy fats in the walnuts.

CARROT AND WALNUT BREAD

For a 13in (32cm) long loaf pan (2 loaves)

1⅓ cups	soy milk, plus extra for brushing
2¼ tsp	active dry yeast
3½oz (100g)	walnuts
2 tbsp	vegan margarine, plus extra for greasing the pan
1lb 2oz (500g)	carrots
2 tbsp	lemon juice
5¼ cups	spelt flour with a high gluten content, plus extra for dusting
½ tsp	salt
1	pinch of fine cane sugar

Time: 30 mins prep + 70 mins proofing + 45 mins baking

1 Gently heat the soy milk in a small pan over low heat. Pour into a bowl, sprinkle in the yeast, cover, and leave at room temperature for about 10 minutes. Then stir until smooth with a balloon whisk.

2 Roughly chop the walnuts and toast them in a dry pan. Add the margarine and let it melt. Peel and finely grate the carrots, then mix them with the lemon juice in a bowl.

3 In a large bowl, combine the flour, salt, and sugar. Work in the milk and yeast mixture, then add the walnut and margarine mix plus the grated carrot. Knead everything until it forms a smooth and supple dough. Shape it into a ball, cover, and leave to proof in a warm place for about 40 minutes, until doubled in size.

4 Knead the dough vigorously once more and shape into 2 small loaves. Put these into a well-oiled loaf pan dusted with flour. Cover and leave for a further 20 minutes. Preheat the oven to 375°F (190°C). Make diamond-shaped incisions in the top of the bread and brush the top with a bit of soy milk. Bake the loaves in the center of the oven for 40–45 minutes. Remove and leave to cool slightly.

TIP:

Fill a small, heat-resistant bowl with water and put it in the oven during baking—this will make the bread even moister.

WINTRY AND CHRISTMASSY

Delicious treats for festive months: fill your veggie kitchen with holiday fragrances and introduce a bit of winter magic. These sensational recipes, packed with nostalgia, are guaranteed to delight young and old alike.

APPLE STRUDEL

Makes 1 strudel (10–12 portions)

Time: 35 mins prep + 30 mins resting + 35 mins baking

For the pastry:

2 cups	all-purpose flour, plus extra for dusting
1	pinch of salt
2 tbsp	canola oil
1 tbsp	vegan margarine

For the filling:

3lb 3oz (1.5kg)	apples (such as Fuji)
6 tbsp	vegan margarine
¾ cup	breadcrumbs
1	juice and grated zest, organic lemon
1¾oz (50g)	raisins
2 tbsp	rum
⅓ cup	ground almonds
⅓ cup	fine cane sugar
1 tsp	ground cinnamon
	salt

Also:

powdered sugar, for dusting

1 Boil some water in a pan. To make the pastry, sift the flour into a pile on the work surface and create a well in the center. Add the salt, canola oil, and ½ cup lukewarm water to the well and use your hands to combine everything to a smooth consistency. Don't overwork the ingredients; otherwise, the pastry will become tough and be liable to tear. Shape it into a ball, brush with margarine, and transfer to a plate. Pour out the boiled water, and leave the pastry to rest for 30 minutes under the upturned warm pan.

2 Meanwhile, for the filling, peel and core the apples, divide into 8 sections, then slice into ¼in (5mm) thick crescents. Melt half the margarine in a pan and cook the breadcrumbs until they are pale brown. Mix the apples with the lemon juice and zest, raisins, rum, almonds, sugar, cinnamon, and salt.

3 Preheat the oven to 400°F (200°C). Melt the remaining margarine and set aside. Press the ball of strudel pastry flat on a kitchen towel dusted with flour, then roll it out with a rolling pin. Lift up the pastry with both hands and stretch it out over the backs of your hands until it is paper thin and measures around 24 × 24in (60 × 60cm).

4 Brush about half the margarine in a thin layer over the pastry. Spread the breadcrumbs over the lower quarter of the pastry sheet, leaving a gap of 1½in (3cm) around the edge. Put the filling on top of the crumbs. Fold the outer edges of the pastry over the filling. Roll up the strudel, using the towel to help you, and place it with the seam edge facing down on a baking sheet lined with parchment paper. Use a brush to carefully remove any excess flour.

5 Brush the rest of the melted margarine over the strudel and bake on the middle shelf of the oven for 30–35 minutes. Remove, leave to cool briefly, and serve while it is still warm. Dust generously with powdered sugar before serving.

TIP:

Warm strudel goes beautifully with cold vanilla ice cream or a delicious vanilla sauce (see p.189).

This simple strudel is perfect for when you need to pull together something quickly, but without compromising on taste. It will win over your family and friends.

SPEEDY POPPY SEED STRUDEL
WITH RUM RAISINS

Makes 1 strudel (10–12 portions)

Time: 10 mins prep + 25 mins baking

For the strudel:

1	store-bought puff pastry (9oz/250g); see pp.14–15
1 cup	ground poppy seeds
⅔ cup	fine cane sugar
¼ cup	breadcrumbs
5 tbsp	rum
4–6 tbsp	soy milk, plus extra for brushing
1¾oz (50g)	raisins, soaked in rum

Also:

powdered sugar, for dusting

1 Remove the puff pastry from the refrigerator 10 minutes in advance. Combine the ground poppy seeds with the cane sugar and breadcrumbs in a bowl. Pour in the rum, then gradually stir in just enough soy milk to create a spreadable paste. This can vary depending on how finely ground the poppy seeds are.

2 Lay the puff pastry on the work surface and spread the poppy seed mixture evenly over it, leaving a gap of 1½in (3cm) all around the edge. After soaking the raisins in rum overnight, scatter the raisins over the poppy seed filling.

3 Preheat the oven to 350°F (180°C). Roll up the strudel from the long edge, then fold in the ends, pressing them together slightly. Lift carefully onto a baking sheet with the seam facing down and brush with soy milk. Bake the strudel in the center of the oven for about 25 minutes. Remove and dust with powdered sugar. Leave to cool completely.

TIP:

To make an almond strudel, replace the poppy seeds with ground almonds and the soy milk with almond milk. Simply leave out the rum and raisins.

CHRISTMAS STOLLEN

Makes 1 large Christmas stollen (15–20 slices)

Time: 25 mins prep + 55 mins proofing + 70 mins baking

For the stollen mix:

4¼ cups	all-purpose flour
⅔ cup	ground almonds
½ cup	fine cane sugar
2 heaped tbsp	soy flour
1	pinch of salt
1 cup + 2 tbsp	soy milk
1–2 tsp	vanilla extract
2¼ tsp	active dry yeast
1 tsp	rum
1¾oz (50g)	candied lemon peel
1¾oz (50g)	candied orange peel
8 tbsp	soft vegan margarine
3½oz (100g)	raisins
3½oz (100g)	marzipan

Also:

3 tbsp	vegan margarine
2 cups	powdered sugar

1 Combine the flour, almonds, cane sugar, soy flour, and salt in a large bowl. Heat the soy milk in a pan over low heat, add the vanilla extract, then pour it into a separate bowl. Sprinkle in the yeast, cover, and leave to proof in a warm place for 10 minutes. Then stir until smooth with a spoon and add to the dry ingredients along with the rum, candied lemon peel, candied orange peel, margarine, raisins, and marzipan. Knead everything until well combined, cover, and leave to proof in a warm place for 45 minutes.

2 Preheat the oven to 350°F (180°C). Line a baking sheet with a double layer of parchment paper to prevent the stollen from becoming too dark on the bottom. Create a loaf shape from the dough using both hands, making a shallow depression lengthwise down the center. Bake the stollen in the center of the oven for 60–70 minutes, turning it halfway through the baking time, until a skewer inserted in the stollen comes out clean. Leave to cool completely on a wire rack.

3 To create the powdered sugar coating, melt the margarine over low heat and brush the stollen all over with it. First, dust the base of the stollen liberally with powdered sugar, then do the same on the top. The stollen tastes best if left for 1 week to allow the flavors to develop.

TIP:

Instead of working the marzipan into the dough, you can give the stollen a marzipan filling. Roll 7oz (200g) marzipan into a log shape and place it in the center of the stollen during the shaping process. Proceed as described in the recipe.

PUMPKIN STOLLEN

For a 12in (30cm) long loaf pan

Time: 12 hrs soaking + 30 mins prep + 75 mins proofing + 1 hr baking

3½oz (100g)	raisins
	rum
10oz (300g)	Hokkaido pumpkin, or small red squash
½ cup	soy milk
3¾ cups	all-purpose flour, plus extra for your hands
¾ cup	fine cane sugar
1 tsp	dried yeast
1	grated zest of organic lemon
1 tsp	vanilla powder
½ tsp	ground ginger
½ tsp	ground allspice
1	pinch of salt
6 tbsp	vegan margarine, plus extra for greasing the pan

1 Soak the raisins overnight in rum. Dice the pumpkin and cook it in a pan with the soy milk over medium heat until soft. Process it to a purée with a hand blender and leave to cool slightly. In a large bowl, combine the flour, sugar, dried yeast, lemon zest, vanilla powder, ginger, allspice, and salt.

2 Melt the margarine in a small pan and stir it into the pumpkin purée. Use floured hands to work the purée into the dry ingredients, kneading everything to create a supple dough. Incorporate the rum-soaked raisins and, depending on how moist or dry the dough is, add some extra soy milk or flour, as required. Cover and leave to proof for about 45 minutes in a warm place.

3 Preheat the oven to 350°F (180°C). Knead the dough once again. Grease a large loaf pan, put the dough inside, and leave to proof for about another 30 minutes. Bake the stollen in the center of the oven for about 1 hour. If the stollen begins to get too brown, cover it with foil. Remove and leave it to cool completely.

TIP:

You can leave the skin of the Hokkaido pumpkin on, as it tastes really delicious. Eat the stollen plain, dusted with powdered sugar, or spread with vegan margarine.

Different German regions have different names for these traditional bun men, including "Weckmann," "Stutenkerl," and "Krampus." No matter the name used, they are usually baked and eaten between Saint Martin's Day and Christmas in Germany.

"WECKMÄNNER" BUN MEN

Makes 6 dough figures

Time: 25 mins prep + 70 mins proofing + 20 mins baking

For the dough:

1½ cups	soy milk
2¼ tsp	active dry yeast
4¾ cups	all-purpose flour
1½ tsp	salt
½ cup	fine cane sugar
7 tbsp	soft vegan margarine
1–2 tsp	vanilla extract

Also:

raisins, to decorate
soy milk, for brushing

1 To make the dough, warm the soy milk over low heat, then remove from the heat. Sprinkle in the yeast, cover, and leave to stand at room temperature for 10 minutes. Combine the flour with the salt and sugar in a bowl. Add the margarine in little blobs and work it in slightly with your fingers until the lumps are no longer visible. Add the vanilla extract. Make a well in this mixture and pour in the milk and yeast mixture. Slowly work the ingredients together to form a supple dough. Knead the dough for 5 minutes, cover, and leave to proof in a warm place for 30 minutes, until it has doubled in size. Then knead it once again.

2 Line a baking sheet with parchment paper and shape little dough figures from the mixture. To do this, split the dough into 6 equal portions, roll each piece into a fairly thick sausage shape, and flatten it slightly. Cut the top of the dough at the sides slightly and round it off to make the head. To make the legs, make a vertical incision at the bottom and pull the two sections apart. Make the arms in a similar manner.

3 Lay the little figures on a baking sheet; press in raisins for the eyes, mouth, and buttons; and brush the dough with soy milk. Cover and leave to proof in a warm place for about 30 minutes. Meanwhile, preheat the oven to 400°F (200°C). Bake in the center of the oven for 15–20 minutes. Remove and leave to cool completely.

TIP:

To make your dough figures a consistent size and shape, it helps to create a paper template to guide you when shaping the dough.

This traditional spiced loaf is wonderfully moist and nutty, with Christmassy flavors that smell delicious before it's even cooked.

MOM'S SPICE BREAD

Makes 4 small 10in (25cm) loaves

Time: 35 mins prep + 12 hrs steeping + 90 mins baking

1lb 10oz (750g)	apples
7oz (200g)	walnuts
1lb 2oz (500g)	raisins
2 tbsp	rum
1 tbsp	vegan cocoa powder
1 cup + 2 tbsp	fine cane sugar
3½ cups	all-purpose flour
½ tsp	baking powder
¾ tsp	salt
1½ tsp	ground cloves
1½ tsp	ground cinnamon
1½ tsp	ground allspice
2 tbsp	ground flax seed

1 One day in advance, grate the apples, including the skin, into a bowl. Add the walnuts, raisins, rum, cocoa powder, and sugar and combine everything thoroughly. Cover the bowl with plastic wrap and leave to steep overnight in the refrigerator.

2 The following day, add the flour, baking powder, salt, and spices. Stir 3 tablespoons of water into the flax seed, leave to swell for a few minutes, then add this to the mix. Knead everything until you have a smooth dough. The dough is very heavy, so it's important to knead in the flour vigorously with your hands to prevent lumps from forming.

3 Preheat the oven to 350°F (180°C). Transfer the dough into 4 1in (25cm) loaf pans and bake in the center of the oven for 80–90 minutes. If the bread starts to get too brown, cover the surface with parchment paper. Remove the loaves and leave to cool completely.

TIP:

This spice bread tastes even more sophisticated if you combine two or three types of apples. If stored in a cool place, it will keep for several weeks, and it can also be frozen very successfully.

CHOCOLATE COOKIE CAKE

For a 11in (28cm) long loaf pan

1 cup	coconut oil
2 cups	powdered sugar
1 cup	vegan cocoa powder
1 tsp	vanilla extract
50	vegan plain cookies
½ cup	white vegan chocolate (optional)

Time: 30 mins prep + at least 2–3 hrs chilling time

1 Melt the coconut oil in a small pan over low heat. Combine the powdered sugar and cocoa powder and add these to the coconut oil in the pan. Add the vanilla extract and use a balloon whisk to mix these ingredients into the coconut oil.

2 Line a loaf pan with plastic wrap and put in a thin layer of the chocolate mixture, smoothing the surface. Top with a layer of cookies, followed by a layer of the chocolate mixture, and continue in this manner until all the cookies and mixture have been used. The final layer should be a chocolate layer smoothed out to create a nice even finish.

3 Put the chocolate cookie cake into the refrigerator to chill for at least 2–3 hours, until it is completely firm. Turn it out onto a board or flat plate and pull off the plastic wrap. If using, melt the white chocolate in a double boiler and spoon over the cake to decorate. Return the chocolate cookie cake to the refrigerator until ready to serve.

"LEBKUCHEN" COOKIES

Makes 50 cookies

Time: 20 mins prep + 30 mins resting + 15 mins baking

For the dough:

3¾ cups	whole-wheat bread flour, plus extra for dusting
1 cup	fine cane sugar
¼ cup	vegan cocoa powder
2 tbsp	mixed spices (cinnamon, ground cloves, allspice, ginger, mace, and ground cardamom)
1 tsp	baking powder
1 cup + 2 tbsp	soy cream
3 tbsp	canola oil
2–3 tsp	vanilla extract
1 tbsp	amaretto

For the glaze:

1 cup	powdered sugar
½ tsp	orange juice
50	whole blanched almonds

Also:

soy milk, for brushing

1 To make the dough, combine the flour, cane sugar, cocoa powder, spices, and baking powder in a bowl. In a separate bowl, combine the soy cream, canola oil, vanilla extract, and amaretto, then add these to the dry ingredients. Knead everything until you have a supple dough, adding a bit more liquid if required, then leave to rest for about 30 minutes.

2 Preheat the oven to 350°F (180°C). Roll out the dough to about ½in (1cm) thick on a work surface dusted with flour and cut out stars, hearts, and other shapes. Place these on a baking sheet lined with parchment paper and brush with soy milk. Bake the cookies in batches in the center of the oven for 12–15 minutes. Remove and leave to cool completely.

3 Make a thick glaze by stirring together powdered sugar, 2 tablespoons of water, and the orange juice. Brush this over the cookies. Put one almond on each cookie and leave to dry on a wire rack. Store in a cookie tin.

TIP:
You can also use lemon juice to make the powdered sugar glaze, and the almonds can be replaced with hazelnuts.

CHRISTMAS COOKIES

Makes 35–40 cookies

Time: 35 mins prep + 30 mins chilling + 15 mins baking

For the dough:

2 cups	chickpea flour
2½ cups	whole-wheat flour, plus extra for dusting
⅓ cup	fine cane sugar
1 tsp	baking powder
½	juice of lemon
1–2 tsp	vanilla extract
2	drops bitter almond oil
12 tbsp	vegan margarine

Also:

3 tbsp	soy milk
1½ cups	strawberry jam
1 tbsp	powdered sugar, plus extra for dusting (optional)

1 Stir the chickpea flour together with 2 tablespoons of water until smooth. In a large bowl, combine the whole-wheat flour, cane sugar, and baking powder. Add the chickpea flour paste, lemon juice, vanilla extract, and almond oil, then add the margarine in blobs and knead everything until it forms a supple dough. Wrap in plastic wrap and leave to rest in the refrigerator for at least 30 minutes.

2 Dust the work surface with flour and roll the dough out thinly. Use circular or Christmas cookie cutters to cut out shapes. In half of these shapes, use a smaller cutter to cut out a design in the center, making sure you leave a border of about ¼in (5mm). Keep rerolling any remaining dough and cutting until the dough has all been used. You should have equal numbers of solid bases and tops with patterns cut in them.

3 Preheat the oven to 400°F (200°C). Line a baking sheet with parchment paper, place the cookies on it, and brush the tops with soy milk. Bake in the center of the oven for 12–15 minutes. Remove and leave to cool completely.

4 Press the jam through a sieve into a small pan. Bring the jam to a boil briefly over low heat. Remove from the heat, then use a spoon to spread it over the cookie bases. If desired, dust the cut-out cookie tops with powdered sugar before setting them on the bases. Leave to dry.

MUESLI COOKIES

Makes 30–35 cookies

Time: 20 mins prep + 20 mins baking

1¼ cups	whole-wheat bread flour
¼ cup	fine cane sugar
1 tsp	ground cinnamon
1	pinch of ground allspice
1	pinch of ground aniseed
⅓ cup	canola oil
½ cup	almond milk
1–2 tsp	vanilla extract
7oz (200g)	muesli of your choice

1 Preheat the oven to 350°F (180°C). In a large bowl, combine the flour, sugar, cinnamon, allspice, and aniseed. Stir together the canola oil and almond milk, then add the vanilla extract. Add these to the dry ingredients and mix until you have a smooth consistency. Carefully fold in the muesli.

2 Line a baking sheet with parchment paper. Use 2 tablespoons to scoop out the mixture into roughly 1½in (3cm) large dollops on the baking sheet, pressing each one down slightly. Bake the cookies in the center of the oven for 15–20 minutes. Remove and leave to cool completely on a wire rack.

TIP:

A convection oven is not suitable for this recipe, as the cookies can easily become too dry and the dried fruit in the muesli is liable to burn.

Vanilla crescents are a great addition to the holiday season—there should be some in every cookie jar. It's important to make them with real vanilla, as that is what gives them their fabulous flavor.

VANILLA CRESCENTS

Makes 30–35 crescents

Time: 25 mins prep + 1 hr chilling + 20 mins baking

For the dough:

2 cups	all-purpose flour
½ cup	fine cane sugar
¾ cup	ground almonds
1–2	seeds scraped from vanilla beans
1	splash of lemon juice and some lemon zest
12 tbsp	vegan margarine, chilled

Also:

½ cup	powdered sugar
1 tsp	vanilla powder

1 In a large bowl, combine the flour, cane sugar, almonds, and vanilla seeds. Add the lemon juice and zest, then add the margarine in little blobs. Work everything together quickly with your fingers until you have a supple, well-combined dough. Wrap in plastic wrap and leave in the refrigerator for about 1 hour.

2 Preheat the oven to 375°F (190°C) and line a baking sheet with parchment paper. Shape little rolls from the dough, bend and taper them into crescent shapes, and lay them on the baking sheet. Bake the crescents in the center of the oven for 15–20 minutes. Remove them from the oven, leave to cool briefly, then dust them with a combination of powdered sugar and vanilla powder while they are still warm.

TIP:

The scraped-out vanilla bean can be used to make delicious vanilla sugar. Just fill a Mason jar with fine sugar and add the vanilla bean. After 7 days, the sugar will have absorbed the flavor.

Spiced cookies are a traditional German recipe made using shortbread. In the past, wooden molds were used to stamp Christian motifs on the cookies. Nowadays, you will find all sorts of other decorative patterns, too.

SPICED COOKIES

Makes about 30 cookies

Time: 35 mins prep + 1 hr chilling + 15 mins baking

1 tbsp	chickpea flour
1¾ cups	all-purpose flour
1 tsp	baking powder
⅓ cup	fine cane sugar
1	pinch of ground cardamom
1	pinch of ground cloves
½ tsp	ground cinnamon
6 tbsp	vegan margarine
1–2 tsp	vanilla extract
⅓ cup	ground almonds

1 Stir the chickpea flour with 2 tablespoons of water until smooth. Sift the all-purpose flour into a large bowl. Add the baking powder, sugar, and spices and mix everything together thoroughly. Add the chickpea flour paste, the margarine in little blobs, and the vanilla extract. Using the dough hook on an electric mixer, combine everything into a smooth dough, gradually adding the almonds. Wrap the dough in plastic wrap and chill in the refrigerator for at least 1 hour (see below).

2 Preheat the oven to 350°F (180°C). Roll the dough out thinly and use a cookie stamp or cookie cutter to create shapes. Place the little cookies on a baking sheet lined with parchment paper and bake in the center of the oven for 10–15 minutes. Remove them from the oven and leave to cool completely.

TIP:
These spiced cookies taste even better if you prepare the dough the previous evening and leave it to chill overnight.

These shortbread cookies are usually made with lots of eggs, but it's not hard to make a vegan version. Most of the ingredients will already be in your pantry.

PIPED SPIRALS
WITH RASPBERRY JAM

Makes 8 spirals

Prep: 40 mins + 15 mins baking time

14 tbsp	soft vegan margarine
¾ cup	powdered sugar, well-sifted
½ tsp	vanilla powder
1	pinch of salt
2¾ cups	spelt flour
⅓ cup	cornstarch
1	jar good-quality raspberry jam (about 12oz/350g)
9oz (250g)	vegan dark chocolate

1 Preheat the oven to 350°F (180°C). Cream the margarine and powdered sugar in a bowl with an electric mixer on its highest setting until light and fluffy. Stir in the vanilla powder and salt. Combine the spelt flour and cornstarch, then stir these in, too.

2 Transfer the mixture to a piping bag with a star nozzle attached. Line a baking sheet with parchment paper and pipe 16 spiral rings. Bake in the center of the oven for about 15 minutes, until the cookies just turn slightly golden but are not too dark. Remove and leave to cool completely.

3 In a small pan, warm the jam over low heat. Remove from the heat and spread a generous quantity of jam over half of the cookie rings. Place the remaining halves on top and leave to set. Melt the dark chocolate in a double boiler. Dip the rings into the chocolate to decorate as desired, then leave to dry on a wire rack. Store in a cookie tin in a cool, dry location.

TIP:
The dough may vary in consistency depending on the flour. If it is too firm, a bit of soy cream can be added to make it softer. If it is too soft, some extra flour will make it stiffer. These spiral cookies are also delicious with a vegan chocolate and hazelnut spread.

NUT WEDGES

Makes 8–10 nut wedges

Time: 25 mins prep + 30 mins baking + 30 mins cooling

For the main mixture:

2 cups	all-purpose flour
½ cup	fine cane sugar
2 tsp	soy flour
2 tsp	baking powder
10 tbsp	vegan margarine
2–3 tsp	vanilla extract

For the topping:

12 tbsp	soft vegan margarine
¾ cup	fine cane sugar
2–3 tsp	vanilla extract
3½oz (100g)	chopped hazelnuts
2½ cups	ground hazelnuts

Also:

4 tbsp	apricot jam
7oz (200g)	vegan dark chocolate

1 To make the main mixture, combine the flour, sugar, soy flour, and baking powder in a large bowl. Add the margarine in little blobs, then add the vanilla extract and quickly knead everything to a smooth consistency. Roll out the dough onto a baking sheet lined with parchment paper. Bring the apricot jam to a boil with 2–3 tablespoons of water in a small pan over low heat, stir until smooth, and brush this over the base.

2 Preheat the oven to 350°F (180°C). For the topping, combine the margarine with the sugar, vanilla extract, and the chopped and ground hazelnuts, until it forms a coherent mixture. Spread this evenly over the base and smooth the surface.

3 Bake the nutty base in the center of the oven for 25–30 minutes. Remove the baking sheet from the oven and leave to cool for about 30 minutes. Slice into ten 4in (10cm) squares, then divide these in half diagonally to create triangles.

4 Chop the dark chocolate into pieces and melt in a double boiler. Dip the tips of the nut wedges into the chocolate and leave on a wire rack to dry.

TIP:

Nut wedges taste great with any kind of nut—for instance, a mixture of walnuts, hazelnuts, and almonds. The combination of ground and chopped nuts gives the cookies their crunchy bite.

FRUIT PUNCH CUBES

Makes 15 cubes (depending on size)

Time: 35 mins prep + 55 mins baking

For the cake mixture:

4¾ cups	all-purpose flour
1¼ cups	fine cane sugar
1 tsp	baking powder
	zest of 1 organic lemon
1½ cups	canola oil
2–3 tsp	vanilla extract
2 cups	carbonated mineral water
	vegan margarine, for greasing the baking sheet

For the filling:

4½oz (125g)	vegan dark chocolate, plus extra for decorating
¾ cup	apricot jam
6 tbsp	fine cane sugar
1	splash of rum

For the glaze:

1¼ cups	powdered sugar
6 tbsp	red wine
¼ cup	rum

1 Preheat the oven to 400°F (200°C). To make the cake mixture, combine the flour, cane sugar, and baking powder in a bowl. Add the lemon zest, canola oil, and vanilla extract. Stir in the mineral water with a spoon and combine everything quickly to a smooth consistency—it doesn't matter if there are a couple of little lumps remaining. Spread the mixture over a greased baking sheet and bake in the center of the oven for about 15 minutes, then lower the temperature to 300°F (150°C) and continue to bake for an additional 40 minutes, until the cake is golden brown and a skewer inserted in the cake comes out clean. Remove from the oven and leave to cool completely.

2 To make the filling, melt the dark chocolate in a double boiler. Crumble one third of the cake into a bowl and combine with the apricot jam, sugar, rum, and chocolate until you have a firm consistency. Slice the remaining cake in half crosswise. Spread the chocolate and fruit mixture over the lower section, replace the top section, and press down firmly. Use a sharp knife to slice the cake into little cubes.

3 For the glaze, stir the powdered sugar into the red wine and rum until smooth, then dunk the little cake cubes into the glaze. If you wish, grate some dark chocolate on top.

TIP:

The consistency of the glaze should not be too thin, so add the liquid gradually to the powdered sugar and stir until smooth. You can also briefly freeze the cubes before glazing, spike them with a fork, dunk in the glaze, then leave to dry in the refrigerator. The cubes can be glazed twice, if desired.

BASIC RECIPES

YEAST DOUGH For a 12 × 15½in (30 × 40cm) baking sheet
Time: 20 mins prep + 55 mins proofing time + baking time

· ·

2¼ tsp dried yeast | 2¼ cups spelt flour with a high gluten content | 1 tsp salt | pinch of fine cane sugar | 2 tbsp olive oil

Pour ¾ cup lukewarm water into a bowl and sprinkle in the yeast. Cover and leave to ferment in a warm place for 10 minutes. Meanwhile, combine the flour, salt, sugar, and olive oil. Whisk the yeast and water mixture, add to the other ingredients, and knead everything until you have a supple dough. Cover and leave to proof in a warm place for about 45 minutes, until doubled in size. Knead it once again, roll out the dough, place it on the baking sheet, and proceed as described in your recipe.

SWEET YEAST DOUGH
For a 12 × 15½in (30 × 40cm) baking sheet
Time: 20 mins prep + 55 mins proofing time + baking time

· ·

3½ cups bread flour | 3 tbsp fine cane sugar | ¼ tsp salt | ½ cup soy milk, plus about 8 tbsp lukewarm soy milk | 1–2 tsp vanilla extract | 2¼ tsp dried yeast | zest of ¼ organic lemon | 4 tbsp soft vegan margarine

Sift the flour into a large bowl. Add the sugar and salt and combine. Create a well in the center. Gently heat ½ cup soy milk in a small pan, then pour it into the well. Add the vanilla extract. Sprinkle the yeast into the milk, then cover the mixture and leave to stand in a warm place for about 10 minutes. Stir this yeast mix into the dry ingredients, add the lemon zest and margarine in little blobs, and knead everything until you have a smooth dough.

TIP:
To make pizza, try putting the dough in the refrigerator for 24 hours to rise slowly, which results in a particularly light texture.

Depending on how the dough turns out, you may need to add more lukewarm soy milk or flour; the result should be a soft, but not sticky, dough. Cover the dough and leave to proof for 45 minutes, until it has doubled in size. Knead vigorously once again, then proceed as described in your recipe.

PUFF PASTRY For a 12 × 15½in (30 × 40cm) baking sheet
Time: 1 hr prep + about 1½ hrs chilling time

· ·

4 cups all-purpose flour, plus some more for dusting | 1 tsp salt | pinch of fine cane sugar | 2⅓ cups vegan margarine

To make the basic pastry, combine 3½ cups flour, the salt, sugar, 2 tbsp margarine, and 1¼ cups water, and knead until smooth with the dough hook of an electric mixer. Wrap in plastic wrap and chill for 30 minutes. For the margarine layer, quickly knead the remaining margarine into ⅓ cup flour, making sure your hands are cold, and shape into an 7 × 7in (18 × 18cm) slab. Wrap in plastic wrap and chill for 30 minutes. Roll out the basic pastry on a floured work surface to create a ½in (1cm) thick slab. Place the margarine layer on top of this slab of pastry. Fold the corners of the pastry in like an envelope toward the center, enclosing the fat layer inside as you do so and pressing the edges firmly together. Roll it out to a size of approximately 24 × 8in (60 × 20cm) and ½in (1cm) thick. Fold one-third of the pastry toward the center, then fold a third of the pastry over this from the other side. Gently press the slab of pastry flat with the rolling pin, first crosswise then lengthwise. Chill for about 20 minutes. Roll out the pastry again to create a 24 × 8in (60 × 20cm) slab. Fold the two narrow sides in to the center, then fold once again to get 4 layers. Roll it out and repeat the initial fold-roll operation. Chill the pastry for 20 minutes, then repeat the second fold-roll operation. Chill for 30 minutes and roll out to create 10 slabs of pastry, each roughly ⅛in thick and 6 × 6in (15 × 15cm). If well wrapped, these will keep in the fridge for about 7 days.

PIE DOUGH For a 11in (28cm) springform pan
Time: 20 mins prep + 1 hr chilling time + baking time

· ·

2 cups all-purpose flour | 1 tsp salt | 10 tbsp vegan margarine

In a large bowl, combine the flour with the salt and add the margarine in little blobs. Work the ingredients together with 8 tbsp water until you have a smooth dough. Wrap in plastic wrap and chill for 1 hour. Line the springform pan with parchment paper. Roll out the dough and lay it in the pan; if required, pull the edges up the sides to create a rim. Follow the instructions in your recipe for working with the dough.

SIMPLE CAKE MIX For a 11in (28cm) springform pan
Time: 10 mins prep + 40 mins baking time

· ·

2 cups all-purpose flour | 2 tbsp cornstarch | ½ cup fine cane sugar | 2 tbsp baking powder | pinch of salt | ½ cup canola oil | ⅔ cup soy milk | 2–3 tsp vanilla extract | ⅔ cup carbonated mineral water

Preheat the oven to 350°F (180°C). In a large bowl, combine the flour, cornstarch, sugar, baking powder, and salt. Stir the canola oil into the soy milk until smooth, add the vanilla extract, and mix into the dry ingredients. Add the mineral water and quickly stir all the ingredients with a large spoon until you have a smooth consistency. Follow your recipe, adding any spices required. Transfer the mixture to your pan and bake for about 40 minutes. Proceed as described in the recipe, maybe topping with some fruit.

PALE CAKE MIX For a 12 × 15½in (30 × 40cm) sheet or a 11in (28cm) springform pan
Time: 10 mins prep + 50 mins baking time

· ·

3¼ cups all-purpose flour | 1¼ cups fine cane sugar | 2 tbsp baking powder | some zest from 1 organic lemon | 1 tsp vanilla powder | 2 tbsp cornstarch | ½ cup rice milk | ½ cup corn oil | 1½ cups carbonated mineral water

Preheat the oven to 350°F (180°C). In a large bowl, combine the flour, sugar, baking powder, lemon zest, vanilla powder, and cornstarch. Mix the rice milk and corn oil and stir into the dry ingredients. Finally, carefully fold in the mineral water with a large spoon. Spread the mixture over the sheet or transfer it into the pan and bake for about 50 minutes.

DARK CAKE MIX For a 12 × 15½in (30 × 40cm) sheet or a 11in (28cm) springform pan
Time: 10 mins prep + 40 mins baking time

· ·

2 cups all-purpose flour | ¾ cup fine cane sugar | ¼ cup vegan cocoa powder | 2 tsp baking powder | 2 tsp baking soda | ½ tsp salt | 1¾ cups soy milk | 1½ tbsp cider vinegar | ⅔ cup canola oil

Preheat the oven to 350°F (180°C). In a large bowl, combine the flour, sugar, cocoa powder, baking powder, baking soda, and salt. In a separate bowl, whisk the cider vinegar into the soy milk and leave to thicken for about 5 minutes, then stir in the canola oil until smooth. Quickly combine the dry and liquid ingredients with a large spoon. Spread the mixture over the sheet or transfer it into the pan and bake for about 40 minutes.

BATTER For 1 portion
Time: 15 mins prep

· ·

2⅓ cups whole-wheat flour | 1 tsp baking powder | 1 tbsp olive oil | 1⅛ cups beer or other carbonated liquid | 1 tsp salt | fine cane sugar | ½ portion vegan whipped "egg whites" (see p.188 for the recipe)

Combine the flour and baking powder in a large bowl. First, add the olive oil, then the beer (or other liquid), and stir everything quickly with a large spoon until smooth. Add the salt and sugar. Carefully fold in the vegan whipped egg whites. Proceed as described in the recipe. For example, for apple fritters, dip the apple rings in the batter, fry in plenty of fat, and leave to drain on paper towel.

MERINGUES For 8–15 meringues (depending on size)
Time: 30 mins prep + 2 hrs baking time

1 portion vegan whipped "egg whites" (¾ cup, see recipe, right) | 1 cup powdered sugar | 1 tsp guar gum | 1 tsp vanilla extract

Preheat the oven to 250°F (130°C). Follow the recipe for vegan "egg whites," right. Sift the powdered sugar into a bowl, add the guar gum and vanilla extract, and mix. Fold the mixture spoon by spoon into the egg whites and beat using an electric mixer on its highest setting. Transfer to a piping bag with a star nozzle and pipe equal-sized blobs onto a baking sheet lined with parchment paper. Let the meringues dry out in the center of the oven for 1½–2 hours. Remove the meringues and leave to cool completely. Store in an airtight container.

COOKIE DOUGH For 25–30 cookies
Time: 35 mins prep + 1 hr chilling time + 15 mins baking time

2 cups bread flour, plus some more for dusting | ½ cup fine cane sugar | 1 tsp chickpea flour | 1–2 tsp vanilla extract | 12 tbsp vegan margarine | 1 cup powdered sugar | juice of ½ lemon | colorful sprinkles, to decorate

In a large bowl, combine the flour and cane sugar. Stir 2 tsp water into the chickpea flour to create a paste, add the vanilla extract, then add to the dry ingredients. Add blobs of margarine and combine everything quickly to make a smooth mixture. Wrap the dough in plastic wrap and chill for about 1 hour. Preheat the oven to 350°F (180°C). Generously dust a work surface with flour (or line it with parchment paper), roll out the cookie dough, and cut out shapes. Place these on a baking sheet lined with parchment paper. Bake in the center of the oven for 10–15 minutes. Remove and leave to cool completely. To make the icing, sift the powdered sugar into a bowl. Stir

in a teaspoon of lemon juice at a time, stirring it into the powdered sugar until smooth. The aim is to create a thick glaze. Spread over the cookies and decorate with sprinkles.

FLAX SEED "EGG WHITES" For 1 portion
Time: 5 mins prep + 30 mins cooking time + 1 hr chilling time

4 tbsp flax seed

Bring the flax seed and 2 cups water to a boil in a pan. Simmer over low heat for 20–25 minutes, until it forms a gel-like consistency. Strain the contents of the pan into a bowl through a fine sieve to separate the gel from the flax seed granules. Chill the gel for 1 hour, then beat it for several minutes with an electric mixer or a food processor on its highest setting to create a neutral-tasting plant-based foam.

GLACÉ ICING For 1 round cake (9½in/24cm springform)
or 1 loaf cake (10½in/26cm long pan)
Time: 5 mins prep

1 cup powdered sugar | 2–3 tbsp lemon juice, water, or some other liquid (juice, syrup, milk, tea, liqueur, coffee, red wine, rum) | nuts, grated chocolate, colorful sprinkles, to decorate (optional)

Sift the powdered sugar into a bowl and add the liquid a few drops at a time—the quantity will depend on the desired consistency of your icing. Stir with the balloon whisk until you have a smooth, very viscous mixture. For icing with a stronger flavor and that is more "opaque," add less liquid. Apply the icing as soon as possible because it sets quickly. Using hot liquid to make the icing helps it bind successfully and gives it a particularly wonderful sheen after it has dried. If you want to add any decorations, this needs to be done soon after the icing has been applied.

TIP:
It's easy to make your own piping bag for decorating: just cut out a triangle of parchment paper, roll it up into a cone (with the point sealed), and fold over the top edge. Fill it half full of the mixture, snip off the tip, and decorate your baked goods in whatever style you like.

FROSTING
For 1 round cake (9½in/24cm springform) or 1 loaf cake (10½in/26cm long pan) or 12 cupcakes
Time: 15 mins prep

12 tbsp soft vegan margarine | about 3⅓ cups powdered sugar | about 4 tbsp juice, jam, or fruit compote, as desired and at room temperature

Cream the margarine in a bowl until light and fluffy, then sift in the powdered sugar and combine. Add teaspoonfuls of the juice, jam, fruit compote, or other flavoring, stirring carefully. The quantity can vary depending on the desired consistency—very runny ingredients need more powdered sugar; more viscous and cohesive ingredients, such as fruit purées, need less. Spread the cake with the frosting.

APRICOT GLAZE
For 1 round cake (9½in/24cm springform pan) or 1 loaf cake (10½in/26cm long pan)
Time: 10 mins prep

4 tbsp apricot jam | 1 tbsp orange juice

Purée the jam and press it through a fine sieve. Stir it into the orange juice in a pan and simmer for about 2 minutes over low heat. Spread the hot glaze over your cake with a pastry brush and leave to dry. Using an apricot glaze gives cakes, tarts, and other baked items a great flavor and keeps them fresh for longer. The icing on a creamy gateau stays in place better if you use an apricot glaze.

VANILLA CUSTARD
For about 2⅓ cups custard
Time: 15 mins prep

⅓ cup cornstarch | 2 cups soy, rice, or oat milk | 2–3 tsp vanilla extract

Stir the cornstarch and a little milk until smooth. Put the remaining milk into a pan and bring to a boil with the vanilla extract over medium heat. Remove from the heat and stir in the cornstarch paste with a whisk. Bring it back to a boil, stirring constantly, until you have a thick custard—the longer it cooks, the thicker it will become.

VANILLA SAUCE
For about 2½ cups sauce
Time: 15 mins prep

2 cups almond milk | 2 heaped tbsp cornstarch | seeds from 1 vanilla bean, plus the bean itself | 3 tbsp fine cane sugar | pinch of salt | 7oz (200g) coconut cream

Take 4 tbsp of the almond milk and stir in the cornstarch with a whisk until smooth. Put the remaining milk into a pan and bring to a boil over medium heat. Add the vanilla seeds, vanilla bean, sugar, salt, and coconut cream and return to a boil, stirring constantly. Remove from the heat and quickly stir in the cornstarch paste with a whisk. Continue to cook until the sauce has thickened. Warm vanilla sauce goes well with strudel and other dishes.

BUTTERCREAM FROSTING
For 1 round cake (9½in/24cm springform)
Time: 15 mins prep

12oz (350g) vanilla custard (see left, cooked until thick) | 12 tbsp soft vegan margarine | ⅔ cup powdered sugar

Allow the thick, cooked custard to cool to room temperature. Meanwhile, cream the margarine in a bowl, sift over the powdered sugar, and stir. Carefully stir the custard into the margarine and powdered sugar mixture. Spread a thick layer over your cake and leave to chill.

CREAM TOPPING
For 1 round cake (9½in/24cm springform) or 1 loaf cake (10½in/26cm long) Time: 10 mins prep

1 pack soy cream, suitable for whipping (10oz/300g), well chilled | 1 tsp cream stiffener | extra ingredients to add flavor and/or color as desired (vanilla extract, cinnamon, vegan food coloring, and so on)

Whip the soy cream using an electric mixer on its highest setting for at least 3 minutes, sprinkling in the cream stiffener as you do so. Beat in any additional ingredients. Use the topping to add the finishing touches to a cake, then leave the cake to cool completely.

INDEX

THE AUTHORS ...

Jérôme Eckmeier has worked at numerous prestigious restaurants both in Germany and abroad since training as a chef and food technician. For several years he has been cooking vegan food and following a vegan lifestyle. His internet cooking show and blog with his new vegan creations are a source of constant inspiration.

Daniela Lais is a freelance journalist and author living between Portland, Oregon, and Hoerbranz in Austria. She has worked for many years in the bakery of the oldest vegetarian–vegan restaurant in Austria and has been vegan for more than 15 years.

... WOULD LIKE TO THANK

Thank you to my wife Melanie (for her patience with me), our kids, our unborn veggie baby, and also my parents. Thanks must also go to: Franz and Traute, Marius and Frauke, the Keller family, Dr. Norbert Knitsch, the Eckmeier clan from the Ruhr region, the guys at Budo Nüttermoor, my sensei Hardwig Tomic, Markus at Little Harbour Tattoo, the German Vegetarian Association (VEBU), Bernd Drosihn at tofutown, Sebastian Bete from the OZ, Erwin and Sandra, Ingo Jäger, Tatjana and Boris Seifert, Brigitte "Sunshine" Kelly, Nicole Bader, Andreas Kessemeier and the staff at Pool Position, Mike Beuger at the law firm WBS in Cologne, Vik and Tina, the team at VHS Leer, the magazine *Vegetarisch Fit*, cinemadirekt Berlin, Keimling Naturkost health food store, Jan Bredack and his family, the team at Veganz, Baola in Munich, Chris from myey.info, Roadhouse Herbrum, and all you rock 'n' roll guys who have supported me in my work.

My thanks go to my parents and all the friends who appreciate my creations and support me. Thanks to Joel, from whom I learned so much American food culture, proverbs, and wisdom, my friends Janet, Steven, Chris, David, and Denise, who have inspired many of my recipes and supported me in so many ways. I thank my community and many friends in Portland, Oregon, the most beautiful city in the world, and in my homeland. Thanks to my friend Janine Favia, from whom I learned a lot. You are a role model for me with your zest for life! Thanks to my publisher DK, to my co-author Jérôme Eckmeier and the VEBU, now proVeg. I thank all people who are committed to herbal nutrition. Last but not least, a very big thank you to the people who support me in everyday life and on my way, no matter in what way. I am infinitely grateful to each of you – without you, this book would not exist.

We are grateful to the following companies for their kind support: Soyatoo! cream, Viana—smoked tofu, Baola, Keimling Naturkost health food store, myey.info, Veganz—We Love Life, and www.alles-vegetarisch.de

Photography Brigitte Sporrer
Food styling Julia Skowronek
Editorial Sabine Durdel-Hoffmann
Design Sonja Gagel
VEBU Coordination Bettina Paul
Title and chapter design Ernesto Kofla

For DK Germany
Publisher Monika Schlitzer
Project manager Sarah Fischer
Production manager Dorothee Whittaker
Production controller Arnika Marx
Producer Inga Reinke

For DK UK
Translator Alison Tunley
Editor Claire Cross
Senior editor Kathryn Meeker
US editor Kayla Dugger
Senior art editor Glenda Fisher
Producer, pre-production Robert Dunn
Producer Stephanie McConnell
Creative technical support Sonia Charbonnier
Managing editor Stephanie Farrow
Managing art editor Christine Keilty

First American Edition, 2018
Published in the United States by DK Publishing
345 Hudson Street, New York, New York 10014

Copyright © 2018 Dorling Kindersley Limited
DK, a Division of Penguin Random House LLC
18 19 20 21 22 10 9 8 7 6 5 4 3 2 1
001–313338–Oct/2018

A catalog record for this book is available from the Library of Congress.
ISBN 978-1-4654-8013-2

DK books are available at special discounts when purchased
in bulk for sales promotions, premiums, fund-raising, or educational use. For details, contact:
DK Publishing Special Markets, 345 Hudson Street, New York, New York 10014
SpecialSales@dk.com

Printed and bound in China

A WORLD OF IDEAS:
SEE ALL THERE IS TO KNOW

www.dk.com